INVESTING IN STOCKS

*Building Wealth and Financial Freedom
through Stock Market Investments
(2023 Guide for Beginners)*

Oswald Beck

TABLE OF CONTENTS

CHAPTER 1

INFORMATION ON THE STOCK

Market stock is a kind of security that implies proportionality.

Having a stake in a corporation. Stocks are mostly bought and sold on stock exchanges, although private transactions may sometimes occur. These exchanges/trades must comply with government regulations, which are intended to protect investors from deceptive activities. Stocks may be purchased via a variety of internet venues.

To raise cash, businesses issue (offer) stock. The stockholder (a shareholder) now owns a piece of the firm and shares in its profits and losses. As a result, a shareholder is regarded a corporate owner. The quantity of shares a person holds in relation to the number of shares the firm is split into limits ownership.

For example, if a firm has 1,000 shares of stock and one person owns 100 of them, that person receives 10% of the company's capital and earnings.

Stock Exchanging Information
Financial gurus do not own firms; rather, they sell the shares that corporations offer. There are several sorts of firms under the law, and some are considered autonomous due to the way they have structured their enterprises. Regardless of the sort of firm, they must eventually record expenses, income, structural changes, and so on, or risk being sued. A firm formed as an "independent," sometimes known as a sole proprietorship, implies that the owner accepts all duties and is personally accountable for all financial elements of the company. A corporation of any kind signifies that the firm is independent of its owners, and the owners are not personally liable for the financial elements of the business.

This distinction is critical because it restricts the commitment of both the firm and the shareholder/owner. If the business fails, a court may order that it be liquidated; nevertheless, your personal assets will not be jeopardized. The court cannot order you to sell your stock, even if the value of your stock has dropped dramatically.

What Exactly Is Trading?
Trading is the fundamental concept of trading one item for another. It is purchasing or selling in this context when remuneration is provided by a buyer to a seller. Within an economy, trade may take place between sellers and purchasers. Overall, trade enables nations to create marketplaces for the exchange of goods and services that would not have been possible otherwise. It is the reason why an American buyer has the option of using a Japanese, German, or American conduit. Because of general commerce, the market is becoming more

competitive, allowing purchasers to get items and services at reasonable prices.

Trading in financial markets includes the purchase and sale of insurance, such as shares on the New York Shares Exchange (NYSE).

Stock/Securities Exchange Fundamentals

Stocks and securities are traded on venues such as the New York Stock Exchange and Nasdaq. Stocks are listed on a certain exchange, which connects buyers and sellers and allows them to trade such stocks. The transaction is monitored in the market and enables purchasers to get business shares at reasonable costs. The value of these stocks fluctuates based on a variety of market conditions. Investors might consider these variables and decide whether or not to buy these stocks.

A market record monitors the worth of a stock, which either addresses the market as a whole or a particular segment of the market. In this respect, you're most likely to hear about the S& P 500, the Nasdaq composite, and the Dow Jones Industrial Average. Data is used by financial advisers to assess the worth of their own portfolios and, on occasion, to shed light on their stock trading judgments. You may also combine your assets into a comprehensive portfolio depending on market data.

Stock Trading Information

Most financial gurus would be well-versed in constructing a portfolio of various financial assets. Experts who desire more movement, on the other hand, are more interested in the stock market. This sort of investing involves the purchase and sale of stocks. People who trade stocks want to utilize market data and events to either sell stocks for a profit or acquire stocks at low prices and sell them later for a profit. Some stock traders are speculative investors, which means they purchase and sell stocks on a regular basis. Others are dedicated investors, making as little as twelve trades every month.

Financial specialists who trade stocks do extensive study as often as possible, dedicating hours each day to watching the market. They depend on specific audits, utilizing instruments to track a stock's developments in order to uncover trading opportunities and instances. Several internet brokers provide stock trading information, such as expert reports, stock research, and charting tools.

What Exactly Is a Bear Market?

A bear market occurs when stock values decline by 20% or more. The phrase "bear market" may be acceptable to progressive financial analysts. Profits in the trading sector usually outlive the average bear market, which is why, during a bear market, clever investors would keep their shares until the market rebounds. This has occurred several times.

When you include reinvested profits and diverse growth, the S&P 500, which contains roughly 500 of the best firms in the United States, has constantly maintained an average of around 7%. That means that if you put $1,000 down 30 years ago, you may have roughly $7,600 now.

Stock market collapse vs. market correction

A crash occurs when commercial value prices drop by 10% or more. It is an unexpected, very steep drop in stock values, such as in October 1987, when equities fell 23% in a single day. The stock market is more vulnerable to market collapses, which may last anywhere from two to nine years.

The importance of progress

It is impossible to eliminate the danger of bear markets, the economy collapsing, or even losing money when trading. What you can do is lessen the impact of these sorts of markets on your investment by keeping a diverse portfolio.

Diversification protects your portfolio against market dangers that cannot be avoided.

If you put a substantial amount of your money into one kind of investment, you're wagering on growth that may quickly convert to loss due to a variety of causes. To mitigate risk, financial gurus diversify by grouping many kinds of stocks together, mitigating the unavoidable probability that one stock could fall, affecting your whole portfolio, or causing you to lose everything. Individual stocks and assets may be combined into a single portfolio. One suggestion: each time you decide to invest, allocate 10% or less of your portfolio to a few stocks in which you believe.

Investing Alternatives

New investors may buy stocks in a variety of methods. If you need to pay extremely minimal costs, you will have to put in more time making your own transactions. If you want to beat the market, you'll have to spend more if you hire someone to trade on your behalf. If you don't have the time or inclination, you may have to settle for less satisfactory outcomes. When the market is doing well, most stock buyers get concerned. Surprisingly, this causes individuals to buy equities at their most turbulent. Obviously, a company share that is underperforming causes concern. As a result, most investors sell when prices are low.

The Stock Exchange's Behavior

The stock market, like other companies, has ups and downs based on how investors adjust their financial pricing in relation to market equilibrium. Stock prices often fluctuate and may have an impact on the stock market, either favorably or adversely. When discussing market equilibrium, investors may become optimists, causing prices to skyrocket, and favoring traders. Similarly, they may become pessimists, causing prices to fall too low, leading to losses and a drop in stock value. This has prompted economists to dispute whether stock markets are necessary and helpful. Multiple causes, according to various economists' interpretations, contribute to these stock market movements.

Some similar aspects have been related to political and financial news from various sources. Another factor is market irrationality, which is heavily influenced by economic news and other market occurrences. Crashing in the stock market is often a bad event when the stock market value declines, resulting in billions of dollars lost by corporations and investors. Crashes are generally caused by fear and loss of confidence, with the most well-known crashes being the Wall Street Crash of 1929, the Stock Market Crash of 2008, and Black Monday in 1987.

Various market experts have developed methods of anticipating how the stock market behaves throughout the years and previous collapses. The approach finds online predecessors based on Google trends searched data about shares using trading techniques. When the search volume is excessive, it implies that there is a possibility of future losses. Similarly, the drop in search traffic suggests that the stock market will stabilize in the following months. The prices of stocks, which are often documented in the form of stock market indexes, therefore change based on the amount of search data. The FTSE, Euronext, and S&P are among the indices.

CHAPTER 2

UNDERSTANDING THE FUNDAMENTALS OF STOCK INVESTING

Before you begin stock trading, you must understand how to choose the right stocks, which requires a thorough understanding of an organization's annual report and financial statements. Determine how to grasp what stock genuinely represents in a business and how to determine the true worth of any stock. This allows you to make smarter investment decisions by avoiding the costly mistake of purchasing an organization's shares when the market has pushed its offer price unduly high in relation to its worth.

Financial Terminology

Throughout the accompanying material, you may come across financial phrases that you may not be familiar with. Without getting into much detail, you'll notice the following words are often used:

Earnings per share: The total organization profit separated by the number of shares is remarkable.

Introducing yourself to the world: Slang phrase when a company plans to go public with its shares.

Short for initial public offering, this is when a company sells a part of its equity for no reason.

Market Cap: An abbreviation for Market Capitalization. The amount of money you would have to spend if you bought every share of stock in a company (to calculate market top, multiply the number of offers by the price per share).

Offer: An offer, or a single regular stock, represents one unit of a financial specialist's ownership in a piece of an organization's advantages, losses, and resources. When an organization divides itself into sections and sells them to speculators for money, it creates shares.

Ticker Symbol: A brief string of letters that refers to a particular stock as it is listed on the stock exchange. The Coca-Cola Company, for example, has a ticker symbol of KO, while Johnson & Johnson has a ticker symbol of JNJ.

Financier: A financial foundation or investment bank that handles the bulk of the administrative work and conducts an organization's initial public offering (IPO).

Growing a Company with Equity
It understands the concept of a company and the stock market while determining how to value a firm. Almost every large corporation started as a small, family-run business and grew to become a financial behemoth. Take a look at Walmart, Amazon, and McDonald's. Walmart began as a single-store operation in Arkansas. Amazon began as an online bookstore in a garage. McDonald's was formerly a little restaurant that no one outside of San Bernardino, California had ever heard of. How did these little businesses grow from modest main-street companies to three of the largest in the American economy? They obtained funds by selling shares in their company.

As a company grows, it has the challenge of accumulating enough capital to support continual expansion. Proprietors, for the most part, have two options for dealing with this. They may either get the funds from a bank or financial speculator, or they can sell a portion of the company to speculators and use the proceeds to support expansion. Organizations often get bank credit since it is usually straightforward to obtain and beneficial to a limited degree. Banks don't often lend money to businesses, and too concerned executives may try to obtain too much, adding a lot of responsibility to the organization's monetary record and harming its exhibition metrics. Factors such as these usually induce smaller, emerging firms to issue shares. They get money to expand the firm in exchange for a small split of possessive control.

Aside from capital that does not have to be repaid, opening up to the world, as is thought when a company sells shares in itself simply because provides the company's executives and owners another tool. Rather than spending money for particular transactions, such as the acquisition of another firm or business line, they may use their own shares.

How Is Stock Distributed?
Take the hypothetical firm "ABC Furniture, Inc." to illustrate how issuing stock works is more probable. A young couple decided to start a company after getting married. This allows individuals to work for themselves and plan their working hours around their families. Because the pair have always had a strong passion for furniture, they decided to create a business in their hometown.

After receiving funds from the bank, they rename their company "ABC Furniture" and begin a new venture. During the first few years, the group generates minimal profit because they reinvest the profits in the shop, acquired additional stock, and remodeled and expanded the building to accommodate the growing quantity of merchandise. After 10 years, the company has grown rapidly. The pair has worked out a way to meet the organization's obligations while receiving more than $500,000 in perks each year. Persuaded that ABC Furniture may also succeed in a few larger adjacent cities, the couple decides to create two further locations. They investigate their options and learn that they need more than $4 million to expand. They opt to fund-raise by delivering value to prospective investors, so they sell shares in their company since they have no desire to acquire cash and must pay obligation and premium installments once again.

The organization contacts a guarantor for the stock offering, such as Goldman Sachs or JP Morgan, who examines its financial statements and determines the worth of the company. ABC Furniture, as previously stated, receives $500,000 in after-charge benefits each year. It also has a book value of $3 million, which represents the worth of the land, building, stock, and other resources after fulfilling the organization's commitment. The guarantor inquires around and discovers regular furniture stock exchanges offered at multiple times the profit of its firm.

This's not making sense to me. Simply said, you would double the organization's $500,000 revenue by 20. This resulted in a market value estimate of $10 million for ABC. If you add the organization's book value, the total comes to $13 million. According to the financier's calculations, ABC Furniture is worth $13 million in total.

As an Example
The young couple, now in their 30s, must decide how much of their company they want to sell. At the moment, they own 100% of the company. The more company shares they sell, the more money they'll get, but they should keep in mind that by selling more, they'll be giving up a larger portion of their ownership. As the company grows, that proprietorship will be

worth more, thus an astute businessperson would not sell more than was necessary. Following the discussion, the couple decides to keep 60% of the offer and give the remaining 40% to society as stock. When the figures are crunched, this means they will retain $7.8 million worth of the company, and since they own a higher portion of the stock, more than 50%, they will now be in charge of the shop.

The remaining 40% of the shares they offered on the open market are worth $5.2 million. The guarantor locates financial experts interested in purchasing the shares and writes the couple a cheque for $5.2 million.

Despite the fact that they own less of the company, the owners' share should grow faster since they have the ability to expand swiftly. ABC Furniture successfully establishes two additional shops with the proceeds from its first public offering and has $1.2 million in actual money left over, after raising $5.2 million but only using $4 million.

Their company performs far and away better in the new branches.

Each year, the two new shops generate around $800,000 in benefits, while the old store generates the equivalent of $500,000. ABC now profits $2.1 million per year from its three outlets. Despite the fact that they lack the agility of a private corporation and the capacity to simply stop shop, their organization is presently valued at $51 million. You would get at this by multiplying their annual net revenue of $2.1 million by 20 (the usual furniture stock variety previously mentioned) and including the organization's most recent book value of $9 million since each shop has a book value of $3 million. The couple's 60% ownership is presently worth $30.6 million in absolute terms.

With this paradigm, it's easy to see how independent companies seem to explode in value when they open themselves to the public. The organization's founders,

one might argue, grew richer with time. The amount they may take from the firm was limited to the benefit produced.
Owners may now sell their shares in the company at any time, quickly generating funds.

This technique serves as the foundation for Wall Street. Every day, the stock market functions as a massive closeout, with ownership in companies such as ABC Furniture being auctioned to the highest bidder. As a consequence of human instinct and sentiments of terror and covetousness, an organization might sell for considerably more than or far less than its true worth. A great financial expert works out how to recognize businesses that are now selling for less than their true value in order to acquire as many offers as possible.

CHAPTER 3

STOCK TYPES

S tock selection is not tough, but it is complex. That is, all of the processes are straightforward, but there are a lot of them. The first thing you should learn about stocks is what they are, what they do, and what they can do for you. Because a healthy portfolio must be varied, each sort of stock may be thought of as a distinct type of building brick. Which blocks you add will be determined by the form you want the ultimate construction to take.

Stock Categories:

1. Ordinary Shares

It's an equity instrument, which means it provides you with ownership of an entity's earnings. Each share represents one voter's interest in the election of the board, which, as you may recall, takes choices about how the profit and shares should be utilized. They are high-risk/high-return investments since there is no market protection, but there are also no middlemen between the shareholder and the percentage of earnings that they own. If the firm fails, the shareholder is the last to be paid, behind creditors, bondholders, and preferred stock owners. This final category leads us to the next.

2. Preferred Shares

Preferred stocks may be thought of as a hybrid of debt and equity. A preferred stock will typically guarantee annual dividend payments in perpetuity. Obviously, if a corporation must liquidate, dividends would cease, but preferred stockholders will be paid the existing share price before regular stockholders.

Furthermore, unlike ordinary stock, preferred stock does not always come with a vote in business decisions. Because the dividends are set, this form of stock is suitable for corporate portfolios that want to balance risk.

3. Stocks with High Growth

These are equities whose past performance shows that they are expanding and will continue to grow faster than the economy in the foreseeable future. This is obviously susceptible to a great deal of fluctuation and variance. What is a growth stock today that might stagnate next week, depending on the company's health and a variety of other factors? Because brokers are always on the lookout for these stocks, they are usually priced at the maximum level the market will tolerate. Their risk estimate is often in the average to the above-average range.

4. Blue-chip (or bellwether) stocks

Blue Chip stocks are the stock market's safe bets. These are generally old firms that have been functioning consistently and paying out good dividends for years or even decades. Their risk profile is modest to fairly low, and brokers often keep them for a lengthy period of time.

5. Dividend Stocks

The key difference between these and other equities is the number of dividends paid out each quarter. This is where they earn their name; 50-80% of the profit is normally distributed to stockholders on a regular basis, and it functions just like any other income. These stocks are often in older, more mature, and slower-growing corporations. The risk is low to moderately low since the share price is not projected to climb dramatically.

That may seem horrible, but it's not the goal of buying these companies; it's the dividend.

6. Value stocks

A "value stock" is one that is underpriced with respect to its potential, which is a rather subjective word. This potential is assessed by examining the company's earnings and other metrics that we'll discuss while discussing how to pick a stock. Once you've mastered those techniques, you'll be able to locate stocks that are a good value for money.

7. Stocks That Change Seasonally

When share prices have traditionally tracked the entire economy, we refer to them as "cyclical." This implies that when times are good, these firms do well, and when times are rough, their fortunes tend to suffer. This category includes companies in areas such as aviation, autos, and construction. The main thing to remember about this sort of stock is that its risk level is rather high in the near term, but since it usually always recovers, that risk is considerably reduced when held for a long length of time.

8. Defensive Stocks

Companies in this category might be seen as the polar opposite of Cyclical Stocks. They are less sensitive to economic upheavals since they operate in sectors that consumers purchase from regardless of the economic situation. This category includes utility, food, and pharmaceutical firms. They are often small but consistent earnings at the lower end of the risk scale. This may alter based on new goods and other circumstances, so don't rule them out of a risk-tolerant portfolio.

9. Speculative Stocks

These are companies that do not have a solid recent earnings history but show potential for other reasons. Some dot-com firms come into this category, as do existing organizations that have had a slump but are now led by new and dynamic executives or are launching a promising product. These are very risky investments, but the payoff may be substantial.

10. Distribute Class

Each share often comes with a percentage of ownership in the firm and one vote in corporate control (generally for the board of directors, which makes decisions regarding how the stock is utilized). In certain situations, a corporation will divide its shares into two classes, one of which will have higher voting power. This helps the organization guarantee that choices are made by a limited group of individuals. It also precludes an outside investor from amassing enough equity to affect a hostile takeover. In this example, the shares would be called Class A and Class B, and their business name would be printed on the ticker with a lowercase letter to indicate this. If the company's abbreviation was ABC, the ticker would read ABCa and ABCb.

Class B stocks are often the company's common stock, with each share entitling the owner to one vote. Class A equities continue to reflect the same proportion of the company's own but would give, say, 10 votes per share.
The third significant distinction is that if the firm goes bankrupt and its assets must be liquidated, Class A shareholders will be paid first, followed by Class B stockholders. It should be noted that all debts must be settled before any of the shareholders are paid.

CHAPTER 4

BROKER TYPES

When it comes to investing in the stock market, you must find the correct broker. If you are a newbie, this is the only option to invest in the market. Brokers will assist you in making sound judgments about how to invest in stocks. A broker is not required to counsel you but will undertake other duties.

Brokers on a regular basis

Regular brokers are individuals whose only business is to purchase and sell stocks or shares on your behalf. This is a work necessity; however, they will not advise you on which stocks to invest in. Some part-time brokers will only invest in the stocks that you advise them to. When you engage these brokers, you may get started in the market on the correct foot. You may also engage independent brokers since normal brokers are not usually attached to corporations. These brokers will charge you for their services, and some may mislead individuals into investing in stocks that will profit them or others. To choose which stock to buy, you should always do appropriate research and due diligence.

Brokers who work on a full-time basis

As previously said, full-time brokers are individuals who are engaged to manage an investor's portfolio. These brokers are skilled and well-versed in the stock market. They do the necessary research to better understand the stocks and assist investors in making profits. Because these brokers know which stocks to invest in, they will advise you on which stocks to buy. You will need to pay a bit more money if you want to hire a full-time broker since they will spend all of their time assisting you. If you are new to investing in the market, you may engage a full-time broker to assist you. These brokers will purchase and sell equities depending on your risk tolerance. Most full-time brokers are unwilling to invest in equities since the trend is difficult to anticipate. Full-time brokers like to invest in major corporations because their stock prices are predictable. If you simply want to invest in equities, hire a full-time broker.

Brokers of Boiler Rooms

Boiler room brokers are those who simply exist to deceive the public. These are the folks you should avoid dealing with. They find traders who are inexperienced and defraud them. These individuals are well-versed in all of the trade secrets and know-how required to influence any stock in the market. When they impact the stock price, they might either raise or reduce demand for that stock. You should be aware of boiler room brokers, who are difficult to discover. These brokers will pretend to be interested in providing you with accurate information, but this is not their intention.

Online Marketers

Online traders are persons who research equities on the Internet. When you engage an online trader, they will invest your assets in market equities based on their internet research. Internet traders might operate for themselves or for a company. These traders research the market and may provide market advice. Online traders suggest that you just deal in equities that are predictable. The danger of such stocks is simpler to comprehend. Because they have greater expertise, these traders will charge you more than conventional brokers. If you are new to trading and want to learn how to invest in stocks, you should start with an online broker. You must be able to tell the difference between honest and dishonest brokers.

Brokers on the ground floor

Floor brokers are those who can only trade stocks from the stock exchange's floor or base. These brokers cannot make their own judgments and must instead obey the commands of their brokers or investors. You are unable to locate a suitable floor broker to assist you with your investment. It is best to avoid using floor brokers to assist you invest since they do not provide sound advice. You should thus avoid seeking a floor broker. You should investigate the many sorts of brokers to choose which one best meets your demands or specifications. They will assist you in selecting the best stocks to invest in.

CHAPTER 5

CONSIDERATIONS

You will almost certainly end up with more than one stockbroker to compare when hiring a stockbroker. At the conclusion of your comparison, you should pick just one, that will offer you all of the services and assistance you will need when you begin trading stocks. The following are some elements that can help you choose the best one:

I) The price

Stock brokers offer different rates for their services. If he provides the services that you need and is a well-known broker, you will choose the one that charges the least amount of money in order to optimize the profits of your investment. Some stockbrokers charge commissions in addition to other fees, so you must examine all of these fees before selecting one stockbroker.

ii) Capabilities as a stockbroker

Expert stockbrokers can advise you on the best types of investments to make to avoid losing money in the long run. If you want a stockbroker to be in charge of buying and selling your stocks, pick the most competent since he will always make the greatest selections for your benefit. Examine the stockbroker's track record to determine which one is the greatest to work with.

iii) Trust This is critical since the stockbroker will manage your account and all of the money generated by your stocks.

Licensed stockbrokers are trustworthy. You may also seek a recommendation from someone who is presently employing a reputable stockbroker to put your mind at rest while entrusting him with your assets. It is usually a good idea to run a background check on the stockbroker you are interested in to ensure that he is trustworthy and respected.

iv) The business or corporation he works for

Many stockbrokers work for a certain brokerage firm, so you should learn more about them before using their services. Check that the firm is respectable, has a strong track record of success, and is well-equipped to handle your money. Because so many individuals are trading in stocks these days, obtaining information on a certain brokerage business or firm will be simple.

v) The kind of services they provide

When employing any kind of service, it is usually a good idea to inquire about how the service provider supports his clientele. Choose a stockbroker who will provide you with high-quality help whenever you need it. Some stockbrokers are known to handle their customers unprofessionally or to be inaccessible at inconvenient times, which is not something you want. Ensure that they provide excellent customer service so that you are always regarded as a valued client.

Different Types of Stock Broker Fees

As indicated above, both full-service and cheap stockbrokers charge a fee to their customers for their services:

a) Commissions: This is the amount paid by the stockbroker who performs your stock purchases and sales. This fee is assessed for each transaction that the stockbroker completes. When compared to a full-service stockbroker, discount brokers charge a reduced commission. Always examine the charges charged by several stock brokers before continuing to deal with them to ensure that you are not overpaying.

b) Asset-based management fees: Instead of collecting commissions, stock brokers will charge you a proportion of your entire assets under their control. Their yearly fees normally do not exceed 2%, so it is not a large sum of money, however, this depends on the stockbroker you are working with.

c) Premier account: Stockbrokers provide premier accounts to investors who seek additional services from their stock investing accounts. You may be charged a fee if you upgrade to this kind of account, but you will be able to enjoy credit cards, bank accounts, and other wonderful services depending on the stockbroker with whom you are working.

d) IRA custody fees: You will be charged for any IRA-related documentation completed by your brokerage. Despite the fact that some stockbrokers waive such costs, they end up billing their consumers on an annual basis.

e) Inactivity fees: These are costs levied to investors who have failed to earn a specified level of fees or commissions as agreed upon with their stockbroker. This implies you must remain active throughout to avoid paying this cost.

Investing in Stocks Without the Assistance of a Stockbroker

When it comes to stock investment, the function of a stockbroker is critical. Stockbrokers are meant to make investors' lives simpler, and the stock market is organized in such a way that it may be quite difficult for an investor to do it himself, however, this does not imply it is impossible. If you are the kind of investor who does not trade regularly, you may wish to save money by selling your stocks directly without the assistance of a stockbroker.

Selling your stocks directly will be a considerably lengthier procedure, which means it will take longer than if a stockbroker assisted you with the transaction. Another thing to keep in mind is that you will have no influence over the stock price. This implies you may be able to sell your equities at a considerably lower price than you expected.

Nowadays, investment businesses enable investors to trade in their stocks without contacting a stockbroker. The function of a stockbroker in today's stock market is gradually dwindling as more customers seek methods to decrease fees while maximizing earnings.

There are many methods to do this:
Check with the transfer agent of the firm whose shares you wish to sell to see whether he can assist you. If he accepts, you will transmit your shares to him directly. In this instance, you will be needed to sign the stock certificates and pass them over to him before agreeing on the price of the stocks and closing the sale. Some transfer agencies may charge a little fee for this, but the majority of them provide such services for free, so you might not be charged anything. The cost of the equities you are selling will be determined by the most recent average share price.

Direct purchase programs do not need the use of a stockbroker. Many firms buy and sell their stock via direct purchase programs or dividend reinvestment, which is a safe method to trade stocks on your own. The plan keeps your stocks in the account at all times and enables you to reinvest your dividends to grow the number of shares you own in that firm. If you wish to sell your shares, you may do so by contacting the plan administrator. In this situation, the cost of stocks will be decided by the most recent average share price.

You are permitted to sell your shares directly to friends or family without consulting a brokerage. You'll need your stock certificates for this transaction. The buyer will simply need cash or a certified check. Simply endorse and sign the shares to the buyer. You may wish to look into additional conditions that the company's transfer agent would demand so that you can close the sale quickly.

Set up an online brokerage account and take complete control of your stock purchases and sales. The internet has brought about several changes in the stock market, this being only one of them. An online trading firm is what you need to look for on the internet. Several online trading businesses will enable you to open an account and begin trading stocks. If you have thoroughly researched stock investing and are certain that you can do it, this is the route to take so that you will never have to deal with a stockbroker again.

If, on the other hand, you are a regular trader in the stock market and want to invest more money in more companies, it is always a good idea to have a stockbroker on hand as his skills may come in useful when you need any type of assistance with your investments.

CHAPTER 6

BASIC ANALYSIS

Fundamental analysis is a sort of financial market study that aims to determine the price of an instrument being analyzed by beginning with the primary factors that might alter the values of an index, currency pair, shares, or any other financial instrument.

The goal is always to profit from your trading operations, so if we consider the price of a stock, we will find those characteristics for which the stock should appreciate or depreciate, and we will position ourselves in the direction of the market that is considered correct based on the analysis. All of this is accomplished via the examination of balance sheet data, economic dynamics, the development of interest rates or the balance of payments, and so on. In summary, a rigorous fundamental type analysis is suggested to purchase a financial instrument when the current price is less than the theoretical, resulting in a capital gain (profit).

It is really quite difficult to anticipate the future direction of prices using the elements mentioned; in fact, this form of study is typically time-consuming and requires particular technical expertise. Time and expertise are required to check and interpret data drawn from numerous information sources. However, this strategy implies that the market is logical and efficient, which it is not always.

When you open a trading platform to trade, remember that behind the figures and complex visuals of software, there are always humans who are the true market participants. And humans, as emotional creatures, are continuously enslaved by their emotions.

Today, technology has advanced significantly; there is artificial intelligence and various types of robots, and we also have something that resembles robots in the trade industry. I'm referring to trading systems or automated trading systems. A trading system linked with automated trading refers to the trading gill that investigates and implements the algorithms that may lead to market trading operations in automatic mode without the need for human interaction. Instead, you have genuine robots that the trader has programmed to execute the work.

So, as such, these robots should fully erase the emotional component of financial markets? Not at all; in fact, I feel that the emotional side is still relevant in the age of algo-trading since trading systems (automated trading systems, programs/robots that may trade in place of a person after being programmed with exact setup) are still built and calibrated by people. As a result, emotions may endure even in systems.

The reality is that we live in the digital era and the age of the algorithm, which also applies to trading and investing. As a result, understanding these new instruments has proven to be crucial. Being aware of elements such as tools, psychology, and behavior is always beneficial in any investing sector. Behind any trading activity, whether by individual traders or institutional investors, there is always the rationale of one or more persons, but most importantly, their emotions.

In this respect, keep in mind that emotions are plainly illogical. Emotions are often the driving force behind actions, such as a purchase or sell transaction on the financial markets.As a result, fundamental market analysis becomes particularly effective for long-term operations (temporal order of months or years), but short-term operations (which are at the mercy of the operator's emotions) may escape this kind of management. Having stated that one of the most important tools to learn and understand is:

Economic Events and Basic Data Calendar
The calendar is always accessible online every day of the week and frequently releases vital data; this tool may be displayed and utilized on many channels of economic news distribution, and it is typically a free tool. The following is an example of an economic calendar:

Time	Cur.	Imp.	Event	Actual	Forecast	Previous
05:00	EUR		Core CPI (MoM) (Dec)	0.4%	0.4%	0.4%
05:00	EUR		CPI (MoM) (Dec)	0.3%	0.3%	-0.3%
05:00	EUR		CPI (YoY) (Dec)	1.3%	1.3%	1.3%
05:00	EUR		CPI ex Tobacco (MoM) (Dec)	0.3%		-0.4%
05:00	EUR		CPI ex Tobacco (YoY) (Dec)	1.2%		0.9%
05:00	EUR		HICP ex Energy & Food (YoY) (Dec)	1.4%	1.4%	1.4%
05:00	EUR		HICP ex Energy and Food (MoM) (Dec)	0.3%	0.3%	-0.4%
2 min	INR		Bank Loan Growth			7.1%
2 min	INR		Deposit Growth			10.1%
2 min	INR		FX Reserves, USD			401.18B
08:00	RUB		Trade Balance (Nov)			12.42B
08:30	USD		Building Permits (Dec)		1.468M	1.474M
08:30	USD		Building Permits (MoM) (Dec)			0.9%
08:30	USD		Housing Starts (Dec)		1.375M	1.365M
08:30	USD		Housing Starts (MoM) (Dec)			3.2%
08:30	CAD		Foreign Securities Purchases (Nov)			11.32B
08:30	CAD		Foreign Securities Purchases by Canadians (Nov)			2.03B
09:00	USD		FOMC Member Harker Speaks			
09:15	USD		Capacity Utilization Rate (Dec)		77.1%	77.3%
09:15	USD		Industrial Production (MoM) (Dec)		-0.2%	1.1%

Image 13: An example of an economic calendar is shown in the picture. The table has columns for the time the

news (or data) was released, the currency, the nation concerned for the news issued, and the effect that the news may have, which is characterized in the picture table by the number of heads of bull. The table's columns continue with the kind and name of the event, data from previous publications for the same event, the value predicted by analysts, and lastly, the current published value. The graphic was made with the help of the economic information website Investing.

As I said in the words before the picture, the economic calendar is available via many distribution methods, including online. This is the first tangible instrument that enables you to keep up with economic and financial market news.

I advise the reader to search for the phrase "economic calendar," access the different sites that provide this sort of service for free, and get acquainted with this instrument, remembering that the calendar of economic and fundamental data headlines will always follow the trader's activities. The investment website is not the only source of real-time data; in fact, using a search engine like Google, you can rapidly find other free news suppliers. The reader's attention should be drawn to the prospect of employing the information instrument for personal trading; after that, each operator will utilize the news site they like to use the economic calendar.

- The data's publishing date and time
- The location or country that is interested in the news
- The extent to which the news has an influence on the markets.
- The data's impact on the kind of incident
- The previous value for that specific data might be a number or a percentage.

- The anticipated value, and so analysts' and operators' expectations

When significant economic news is released that has a significant emotional and functional influence on the market, there is frequently an increase in volatility or a major "swing" in prices. This may result in rapid and unexpected profits, as well as swift and unpleasant losses. When reading fundamental data, it is important to understand the market's anticipatory qualities; that is, the price may rise awaiting data that is expected to be favorable.

As a result, the price may fall back to previous levels. This is heavily influenced by the expectations for that sort of news, and hence by the value predicted by the economic calendar. This is certainly not a hard and fast rule. The above line might be reduced as follows: "Buy when the trading community anticipates a positive outcome and sell when the news becomes public."

However, as with any trading and investing, this is not a hard and fast rule that can always be followed; otherwise, it would be much too simple to get wealthy by trading on the stock market. Online trading on financial markets is one approach utilized to obtain Financial Freedom; in reality, if you understand the mechanics that underpin this business system, you may also employ operability that needs minimal effort. This proves to be true in terms of the structuring activities that develop private traders for his firm. Furthermore, it is now possible to commit the management of your trading account to automated algorithms, robots that may be created by the trader or acquired from skilled industry specialists.

It is difficult to earn money with trading since it is an activity that needs continual updating and deepening; this sort of activity may not be ideal for everyone; yet, the truth remains that with trading, you may make a lot of money! The distinction is that the information refers to training and personal expertise rather than information on which tool to purchase or sell (the so-called "inside information"). In the age of the information revolution, and hence the digital revolution, time and money invested in training provide the highest results. In reality, courses and books provide a competitive edge that separates those who can and those who cannot accomplish anything.

CHAPTER 7

TECHNICAL ANALYSIS

Simply said, technical analysis is a strategy, process, or instrument used by investors to forecast and forecast the price movement of a company based on market data.

Technical analysis of trends and stocks may also be defined as an examination of prior market data, including volume and price. The primary goal of the study is to gather the information that will aid in forecasting predicted market behavior. Traders and investors are convinced that the price of precious metals is a reliable predictor of future performance.

There is a concept that lends support to technical analysis. The security seems to properly reflect the aggregate sale and purchase of equities in the markets by traders, investors, and other stakeholders. This implies that technical analysis offers a reasonable and reasonably accurate market price for a stock or other investment.

The goal of technical analysis
The primary goal of technical analysis is to forecast the predicted price movements of stocks and trends and to offer important information to investors, traders, and other market participants so that they may trade effectively.

As a swing trader, you will use technical analysis to analyze the numerous charts you will be utilizing. You will utilize several tools on the charts to assess the probable entry and exit points for a specific trade.

Technical Analysis Influencing Factors

Technical analysis may be used on a wide range of instruments, including Forex, stocks, futures, commodities, indexes, and many more. A security's price is determined by a number of factors. Volume, low, open, high, close, open interest, and so on are examples. These are also referred to as market activity or price data.

When practicing technical analysis, we make a few assumptions as traders. However, keep in mind that it is only valid in cases where the price is only a function of demand and supply. If other variables may substantially impact prices, the technical analysis will fail. The following assumptions are often made concerning securities under consideration.

There are no manipulated price movements: Distributions, dividends, and splits are common causes of artificial price swings. Such fluctuations in stock price may significantly affect the price chart, making technical analysis difficult to apply. Fortunately, this is something that can be fixed. As an analyst, all you have to do is make modifications to past data before the price changes.

The stock is very liquid: Another key assumption made by the technical analysis is that the stock is very liquid. Volumes need a high level of liquidity. When equities are actively traded due to liquidity and volume, traders may simply enter and exit deals. Stocks that are not widely traded might be difficult to trade since there are few vendors and buyers at any one moment. Furthermore, equities with minimal liquidity are often underpriced, sometimes at less than a cent per share. This is problematic because investors may influence them.

Trend: If you want to trade based on trend, you want to follow the herd when it comes to trading and earn a profit on volume along with everyone else. Trends may go up or down, with evidence of an upward trend including higher-than-average lows, and indicators of a downward trend including lower-than-average highs. Whatever the current trend is, the sooner you can identify it, the more you can benefit from it in the long run.

At that time, you should find that maintaining your selected position is a reasonably straightforward thing until the trend reverses. Because a trend trader never knows when the trend may reverse on them, it is critical to constantly utilize carefully controlled stops to guarantee that your gains do not evaporate at the first signals of a reversing trend.

This form of trading is likely to produce a considerably bigger number of lost transactions than other techniques, but the individual winnings are likely to be larger as well. This, in turn, implies that if you don't want to deal with a lot of risk management difficulties, you'll probably feel more at ease trading based on the range instead. A trend-following transaction should never account for more than 2% of the entire amount of cash you want to trade with. Furthermore, it is critical to consider your liquidity to avoid being abruptly in over your head. Keep in mind that it is nearly always wiser to accept a lesser profit now rather than risk it all on something that might knock you out of the game entirely.

Understand the fundamental assumptions: Technical analysis is all about determining the relative worth of a certain transaction or underlying asset by using accessible tools to uncover otherwise unseen patterns that, ideally, few other people have observed. When it comes to performing technical analysis correctly, you will always need to assume three things. First and first, the market eventually discounts everything; second, trends are always a good predictor of price; and third, history is sure to repeat itself given enough time.

When it comes to examining the present state of things both within and outside the market, the technical analysis argues that the current price of a given underlying asset is the only accurate statistic that counts. This is because everything else about the market has already been factored through the price to bring it to where it is today, so studying it in relation to the entire status of the market should give you all of the information you want.

Furthermore, technical analysis keeps true the notion that the current value of an underlying asset changes depending on the established trend, which means it can be monitored as long as you know what to look for. This implies that once a pattern has been discovered, it is only a question of waiting for it to reappear before you can capitalize on it. Statistically, it is always more probable for a trend to repeat itself than for a new trend to emerge out of nowhere or for a trend to reverse suddenly.

CHAPTER 8

TECHNICAL INDICATORS TRADE INDICATORS

This is a trading measure or gauge that enables price analysis and delivers trade signals. Indicators provide trade signals to traders, alerting them when it is time to trade. Day trading indicators should not be utilized as the only strategy. To make it a viable trading tool, it should be utilized in conjunction with a well-designed layout. Having several trading indicators, regardless of the kind of transaction, may result in inconsistency with trading choices owing to the intricacies involved. Keeping things simple may be the key to making straightforward and less stressful trading choices.

As a result, trading indicators should not be regarded as the only trading approach. However, employing indicators in conjunction with other trading factors may be beneficial. Getting rid of the many indications allows traders to take a more straightforward approach to the market.

The Function of Technical Indicators

- Determine the trend's direction.
- Determine the market's momentum or lack thereof.
- Determine whether or whether the market is expanding.
- Get the volume to see how popular a market is among traders.

The problem is getting the same kind of indicators on the chart that convey the same information. This is because you may provide contradictory information or get more information than you can handle. The fundamental disadvantage of most indicators is that, since they are derived from price, they delay the price. There are principles for determining effective indicators for day trading, swing trading, and position trading. This includes, among other things:

- The most basic concept is to use one trend indicator, such as a moving average, and one momentum trading indicator.
- Before deciding on the trade indicators, you will employ on your charts, make sure you understand the boundaries you wish to study. Then, understand the indication you choose in terms of how it works, the calculations it does, and the implications it will have on your trading choices.
- Indicators only function if they are properly integrated into the trading strategy. Some indicators, such as MACD and CCI, excel at computing data. Others, such as the alligator indicator, are quick to reveal a market that is moving and ranging.
- Other indicators will provide direction as well as trading entry and exit signals. The use of a simple indicator in conjunction with a well-planned trading strategy based on back, forward, and demo may put you ahead of trades using numerous intricate indicators.
- Netpicks provides solutions for testing trade strategies, trading systems, and trading indicators.

The Risk of Optimization

There is an impediment or barrier while looking for trading indicators that work for one's trading style and trading strategy. Most systems supply conventional indications that have been fine-tuned to represent prior performance. This is a disadvantage since it does not account for market movements. Using the usual settings for all indicators aids in avoiding the over-optimization trap, which allows a trader to avoid focusing on today's market development and missing out on the future.

Technical Trading Indicators That Work

A trader should test numerous indicators independently before combining them for day trading. One may end up with 3-5 excellent ones that are evergreen and opt to switch off based on the market or asset trading on that given day.Regardless of the form of transaction, day, Forex, or future, the aim is to keep the indicators basic. Use one indication per category to minimize repetition and attention.

Indicator Combination

Combining pairs of indicators on the price chart helps in identifying entry opportunities for trades. A notable example is the use of RSI and moving average convergence to propose and strengthen a trade signal. When selecting sets, it is critical to choose one indication that is regarded as a leading indicator and another that is considered a lagging indicator. Leading indicators provide indications before the forms for entering the trade are completed. In contrast, lagging indicators reveal signs after the formation has occurred. As a result, trailing indicators may validate leading indicators and prevent traders from trading on false signals. It is strongly recommended to choose a variety of pairings that comprise indications of various sorts rather than the same type. Observing a mixture of the same sort of indicators makes little sense since they will still provide the same information.

Several Indicators
Using numerous indicators improves trading signals but may increase the likelihood of detecting erroneous signals.

Indicators of Improvement
Knowing an indicator's flaws is critical for determining if it sends a lot of false signals, fails to signal at times, or signals too late or too early. Knowing these facts about the indicator will help you choose what it is best suited for. You may discover that the indication is more suited for Forex than stocks, despite the fact that you believed it was unsuccessful. This may assist you to determine whether to exchange the indicator for another or just modify how it is computed.By refining an indication, you may make it operate better for you and identify the optimal indicator for various sorts of trading.

CHAPTER 9

IDENTIFYING UNDERVALUED STOCKS

To locate cheap stocks, you must go through three basic steps: Perform a preliminary analysis of numerous equities to see if they satisfy your investing requirements. Create a shortlist of equities to investigate and assess further based on your preliminary review; and Investigate your chosen stocks in further depth by attentively scrutinizing their financial details.

The internet has made it much simpler for investors to get free financial information about firms in which they are interested. Many websites now provide vast databases of financial data, such as audited financial statements, news announcements, business reports, stock prices, and profits per share, such as Edgars and Sedar.

However, with the deluge of data, how can you know whether a certain stock is now being sold below its intrinsic value? Here are only two of the financial measures to consider when determining a stock's intrinsic value:

P/E (Price/Earnings) Ratio
Financial experts will quickly tell you that a specific company is presently trading for "x-times earnings"-20-times earnings or 10.5-times earnings. This signifies that the current market price of the stock is 20 times more than the company's profits per share. The idea is to locate equities with very low P/E ratios since this

indicates that the corporations are selling their stocks at reduced rates.

Yield on Earnings

Earnings yield is the inverse of the P/E ratio. As a result, a corporation with a P/E ratio of 20 has a 1/20 or 5% earnings yield. If value investors seek low P/E ratios, earnings yield is the inverse (i.e., value investors want equities with greater earnings yield relative to other businesses in the same sector).

In addition to the quantitative analyses outlined above, you must also conduct qualitative assessments to have a deeper understanding of a company's intrinsic worth.

The appraisal of the company's "insider purchasing activity?" is one of these qualitative analyses. You're interested in learning what the company's executives (senior managers, officials, directors, and other key investors) are doing with their stock holdings.

These insiders, particularly senior management and the board of directors, have "inside" knowledge of their own company's activities. As a result, if you see them eagerly purchasing their company's shares, you may safely assume that the company's operations are heading in the right direction.

However, don't leap to conclusions if an insider sells his or her stock ownership. It does not necessarily imply that the firm is on its way to bankruptcy or hard times. For all you know, that specific director or top manager is in desperate need of more funds to cover personal expenses. However, you may begin to worry about the company's future prospects if numerous insiders decide to sell the majority of their stock holdings. When you see the such circumstance, you should do more research to determine if the organization is in trouble.

"How will I know when a company's board of directors or senior management is buying or selling stocks?" you may wonder.

Don't worry, the Securities and Exchange Commission (SEC) has made it simpler for investors to learn about this information by requiring insiders to declare their purchases to the SEC within two business days of the transaction. This information is then readily accessible on the official SEC website.

The Fundamentals of Value Investing

As previously said, if you want to be successful in value investing, you must be willing to do some serious reading and research.

You do not need a degree in finance or accounting, but it will be very beneficial if you make an effort to master the fundamentals of accounting so that you can correctly examine and comprehend financial accounts. Remember that you do not acquire a stock because its financial numbers appear good or because you just learned that its current market price has decreased significantly. To assess if a stock is a smart investment or not, you must depend on more than just accepting what you see at face value. To be effective, you will need to employ common sense and critical thinking abilities.

Aside from financial ratios and insider purchase activity, you should spend some time asking and answering the following questions:

What do you anticipate the company's operations will look like in five, 10, or even twenty years? Will the corporation be able to consistently expand its revenues by selling more or raising its prices? Will the corporation be able to maintain an effective operation by tightly controlling the costs of products sold and operational expenses? How often do they sell or shut down non-profitable divisi ons or subsidiaries? How powerful is the firm in its industry? Are they among the market's leaders? Do they have more powerful rivals?

As you gain expertise, you will understand what additional questions to ask. Once you have the answers, you may use them in conjunction with financial ratios and insider buying activity to decide whether or not a specific company is a suitable investment.

To increase your chances of success in value investing, it is best to buy stocks from firms you are familiar with.

This is the approach that enabled Warren Buffett to profit handsomely from his stock purchases. If you have always worked in the airline sector, you might claim to have a thorough understanding of the industry and the firms that operate inside it. Because you purchase clothing, groceries, and home goods regularly, you are definitely familiar with the retail business.

Another strategy used by successful value investors is to buy stocks in firms that have been producing goods or providing services for a long time and have a strong likelihood that their goods or services will continue to be in demand. These firms cannot be identified merely by reviewing their financial data. You will need to use critical thinking skills to identify whether firms belong to this group. As an example, consider the Coca-Cola Company. Coke products have been extensively accepted across the globe for many decades, and many people predict that they will continue to be popular for a long time. You may see how other firms you are acquainted with have evolved over time. It is also excellent if you can do an examination of the firms' management styles to see how successful their corporate governance is in guaranteeing that the companies can prosper in both good and bad times.

Remember that value investors are long-term investors who do not make careless and arbitrary investing selections. They spend their time researching and evaluating a firm before investing their money in its shares. It is never enough to just look at stock market values and read short commentary from financial professionals.

CHAPTER 10

WHO ARE YOUR PARTNERS?

Before you may invest in the stock market, you must first create an account with a broker. The problem is that, with so many brokers urging you to join up and invest, how can you choose the broker that would best meet your needs? Make certain that your broker passes this fundamental so that you get the best investing or stock trading experience possible.

Banking

Check the deposit and withdrawal options. It is not uncommon to encounter brokers that employ many alternatives when depositing but just have a few options when withdrawing. Before you can initiate your withdrawal, a broker will usually need a copy of your identification documents. Take note of how many days it will take your broker to receive your payment in full from the moment you request it.

Minimum Deposit and Maximum Withdrawal Please keep in mind that a minimum deposit is necessary. Some brokers demand a minimum deposit of $250, while others may accept a deposit of as little as $25.You'll also need to understand the minimum and maximum withdrawal amounts. It is typical for a broker to impose a minor fee in addition to a withdrawal fee. If you want to make a number of withdrawals in a given week, you should be aware of the withdrawal fee.

Account Demo

A free sample account must be provided by your broker. This is a great way to practice trading in a real-time stock market setting without risking any money.

Charges

These costs are normally minor, but they may add up quickly, especially if you make a lot of deals in a short period of time. Make careful to evaluate the many brokers you discover online and choose the one with the lowest costs.

Platform for Trading

Every online broker will provide you with a trading interface via which you may buy and sell stocks with a few mouse clicks. Your broker should give you a properly designed platform that includes beneficial features. The best brokers will supply you with free stock market data or information to aid you in making the best financial investment choice. If you want to apply technical analysis, your broker must also supply you with graphs and charts.

Restriction on Trade

In addition to limiting how much you may trade; your broker should not restrict how you trade. Some brokers would demand you to contact them first before purchasing stocks via the site, as though you need their permission for whatever transaction you make. Some brokers may even limit the number of stocks that you can sell or acquire. You should avoid these brokers. You should only engage with a broker who will allow you to make an investment on your own. It should also enable you to trade as many stocks as you like. Trust Rating, of course, you must only engage with a recognized and trustworthy broker. When you open an account with any broker, be sure to read the comments left by other investors. An easy approach to accomplish this is to open your preferred internet browser, type the broker's name into the search box, and then add the term ratings. When you press the Enter key, you will see a list of sites that will most likely include the ratings for your chosen broker. Similarly, pay attention to the dates when the current comments were completed. Be cautious if the most recent good assessments were issued more than a year ago. The management team and even the broker's strategy will change from time to time.

Mobile Function

In addition, the broker will give you a mobile platform. This assures that you will be able to manage your portfolio and save using just your mobile phone. When using a desktop computer, the procedure should be as simple as you are. Don't worry; brokers with great ratings always have a mobile feature. One of the reasons customers choose individual brokers is the availability of a mobile option.

Customer Service

Check to see whether the broker offers live chat on the web. If the broker can only be contacted by e-mail, see how quickly the broker responds and how efficiently the broker handles the order. Ideally, the customer help should be able to respond to your queries within 24 hours!

CHAPTER 11

PURCHASING YOUR FIRST STOCK

Regardless of the higher-than-average volatility, when you acquire stock and earn the legal right to participate in the venture's revenues and losses, your money may grow in ways that are absurd with securities, store authentications, or, at times, even land. For newcomers, one of the most common questions is how to purchase stock; the mechanics of really getting your hands on that piece of property that qualifies you for dividends that are instantly saved or delivered to your family so you can enjoy the rush of passive income.

There are many ways to acquire stock, each with its own set of advantages and disadvantages, such as valuation and liquidity considerations. Some well-known possibilities may help you improve the overall layout of the property and be more informed to make value-securing decisions.

The most efficient way to purchase stock in a regular, taxable brokerage account
If you need to acquire shares without any restrictions, beneficial tax situations, or commitment constraints, the most straightforward approach is to create a brokerage account. Choosing a specific brokerage house includes a few considerations, for example, whether you require a full-administration broker or a rebate broker who simply executes your stock exchanges at the absolute lowest costs, however nowadays it is as simple as taking

five minutes to complete a series of inquiries on the web.

Assume you wanted to create an account with Charles Schwab & Company, the largest broker in the United States. You would complete the online application by providing your name, residence, government disability number, job data, and any further information required, such as edge obligation capacity or stock option trading advantages. You would next send in the $1,000 basic record equalization or, instead, seek $100 monthly direct stores or electronic scopes from Schwab financial records.

When you opened your brokerage account, you would notice the money saved and halted, waiting for you to do anything with it. You would go on to the website, input the ticker symbol of the company you wanted to acquire, enter the number of shares you wanted to buy, and then provide the exchange a couple of snaps once you had reviewed the details. Generally, you'd see the stock saved into your record and the money taken out within a second or two. You'd get an exchange confirmation archive a few days later.

When the organization made a profit, it would be directly deposited into your brokerage account. If the business ever had a tax-exempt side project or split-off, those shares would be preserved in your brokerage account as well (for example, Chipotle Mexican Grill was separated from McDonald's, while Allstate Insurance was spun off from Sears).

The most efficient way to invest in a stock is via a Roth IRA, Traditional IRA, SIMPLE IRA, SEP-IRA, or other similar retirement accounts.
The path to purchasing stock in a Roth IRA is, for all intents and purposes, identical to purchasing stock in a conventional, assessable brokerage account. If your IRA is kept with a brokerage business, you follow the same

procedure. The difference is in how the charges are handled and the amount of fresh money you may contribute each year.

For example, if you are 49 years old or younger, you may contribute $5,500 to a Traditional IRA, and if you are 50 years old or more established, you can contribute $6,500. For as long you go below as far as possible as a consequence of your conjugal status for the year, you may disregard these obligations as if you never brought in the money. In the meanwhile, dividends and capital gains earned while investing in stock within a Traditional IRA are completely tax-free, with a few exceptions. When you go to draw the money out of the record, you pay a standard income fee on the amount pulled back.

If you try to withdraw the money too soon, you will be subject to a 10% penalty fee unless you fulfill one of the eight exclusions. The most efficient way to buy a stock is via a Direct Stock Purchase Plan (DSPP) or Dividend Reinvestment Plan (DRIP).Consider a situation in which you would prefer not to create a brokerage account.

You've entered the realm of karma. Many firms, especially large blue-chip stocks, provide programs that allow you to acquire stock directly from the company's exchange specialist for free or at a heavily subsidized rate. Consider Exxon Mobil, a more evolved cousin of John D. Rockefeller's oil empire. It enables an instant stock purchase plan via a company named Computershare. Potential investors who establish a record with $250 or agree to have $50 deducted monthly from a checking or bank account may purchase the shares with no commission.

Surprisingly, the structure supports partial stock purchases, so every cent goes to work for you, the investor, even if you don't have the exact sum to receive a complete offer at some random moment.

When you apply online, you may choose whether you want your profits direct deposited into your checking or bank account or reinvested in further shares of stock.

Choose with caution. While there is no set-in-stone answer—everything is dependent on your own financial circumstance and the resulting execution of the stock itself—there is a significant difference between reinvesting and not reinvesting your dividends over long periods of time in case you're fortunate enough to wind up possessing a truly extraordinary endeavor.

CHAPTER 12

MARKETING

It is also critical to selling a stock at the right moment. The entire objective of keeping a careful eye on your chosen stocks is to be completely informed of their market performance. It is true that firms with good fundamentals often outperform in the long run. The explanation is simple: the corporations want to expand. There is a whole system in place that is attempting to earn a profit, and as a consequence, even your money invested in that stock makes a profit.

This, however, may not be true for every company endeavor. There may be instances when a corporation that has been doing everything correctly begins to go downhill. There might be several causes for the company's demise.

Management concerns might contribute to the road to self-destruction. Various government laws and limitations might also make it harder for the firm to operate. The causes for a company's demise might range from lengthy and nasty litigation to superior items on the market. It is your job as an investor to keep a careful eye on your investment. You'll need to stay up to date on news about that industry and, in particular, that firm.

First, there is the Value Judgment.
When you know that the value of the stock is about to fall or has already begun to fall, it is critical that you leave the stock and square off your position as soon as possible. It is critical that your choice to sell a stock is not a knee-jerk response. You must realize that many individuals want to square off their holdings in a

fundamentally strong firm the moment they hear anything negative about it. Many times, there is nothing meaningful in such chatter, and organizations recover quickly from the first shock response. However, if you attempt to sell a stock while many other investors are doing the same, you will suffer a significant loss. Remember that the market operates on a demand-and-supply basis.

If a company's fundamentals are excellent but its stock price is falling due to random news or market manipulation, such periods are favorable for purchasing rather than selling. However, if you have a compelling cause to feel that anything is wrong with the company's fundamentals or that something is occurring that would harm the company's prospects in the long term, it would be prudent to sell before the market panics. Your judgment should be based on facts rather than emotions.

Second, there is the Order Judgement.
The next step is to decide what kind of order you wish to place. You may place orders as a market order or a limit order, just as when you buy.

Market Order: If you believe that anything is really wrong with the firm and that a panic-like scenario is possible, it is best to depart as soon as possible. You will be able to square off all of your holdings in that stock at the market rate and will not have to wait long. If you place your order 'after hours,' it will be processed at the start of the following working day at the current prices.
In such a case, you will have no influence over the rates, and whatever the rate is at the time of opening, your orders will be executed at that price.

Limit Order: Use this form of order if you don't believe there's anything wrong with the firm but wish to record profits for another reason. The limit order option provides you with more control over the price you will get.

When you submit your sell order, you may be required to fill out more information on the trading site.

The following information is required:

The number of shares you want to sell: You may either square off your whole investment or rebalance your stock position by selling a few stocks in this company. Enter the exact number of shares you want to sell.

Order kind: In this section, you must specify what kind of order you want this to be. This indicates that you wish to place a market or limit order.

Time in Force or Order Expiry: The next item you must enter is the 'time in force' or order expiry. This clearly defines the time frame for which your order is valid. This is a feature designed to offer you more control.

The following are some of the words you may come across:

Day: This suggests that your current order may be excellent for the day, but you may want to try a new price or technique the next day. If you put this order and the deal is not performed on the same day, you must place a large order at the following market opening.

valid till Cancelled: You may also place an order that is valid for as long as it takes to execute or until you cancel it. This frees you from having to place the bid for that stock repeatedly.

Immediate or Cancel: You may also use this category to place an order to sell your shares instantly. However, any unmet portion of the order will be immediately canceled, and you will have to bid on it again if you wish to square it off.

Fill or Kill: This sort of command is used to square off a big position at once. You may place an order, but it will only be executed if your whole position in that stock is squared off.

On the Open: This kind of order will be executed when the market opens. You will not be able to influence the price at which it is filled. It will be heavily influenced by the market's first reaction to that stock price.

On the Close: This kind of order will be fulfilled at the closing price of the market.

CHAPTER 13

SCAN STOCKS AND CREATE A WATCH LIST

You can only scan stocks as quickly as you can input them into your terminal. This delay in getting information often results in lost chances that may have brought significant gains if you had only observed the setup developing early enough.

This capability is highly recommended since it may find lucrative trading chances early enough for you to take advantage of them. The code I'll supply is essential to the think or swim platform, but the fundamentals will be the same regardless of the analytic program you choose. I urge you to study the information, understand why I set up my filters in the manner that I do, and apply the ideas to your own trading approach.

The first step in building any kind of scanning feature is to construct a well-organized watch list of equities in which you are interested in trading.

As of this writing, I have 230 stocks on my watch list. Each of these stocks has been hand-picked to have the right components in place, making them simple to trade. When it comes to trading stocks, I look for factors like volume, volatility, and stability. It will be difficult to enter and exit positions if the volume is low; the greater the volume of the stock, the simpler it is to establish a new position or trade over current shares to someone else. I usually only trade equities with an average volume of 800,000 shares traded during a 14-month period.

Volatility is the second thing I look for. Volatility in financial instruments is defined as their propensity to vary. Volatile stocks will have big price swings, providing for higher profit potential, while non-volatile companies will trade in a relatively narrow price range, making substantial gains impossible to extract. I utilize a stock's Average True Range (ATR) to calculate volatility. ATR is just the average difference between a stock's low and high of the day over a particular time (I measure ATR over 14 trading sessions). It is vital to understand that ATR is a dynamic variable that varies on a daily basis. Stocks move in cycles where their ATR moves from low too high to low, generally matching with volume.

As a general guideline, I will only trade equities with an ATR of 2% or above. That is, at any moment, the gap between the low and high prices of the trading day will be 2% or more.

The last thing I look for is consistency. Most individuals define stability differently than I do. When I say I'm looking for stability, I'm referring to the Bid-Ask spread. A stable stock has a respectable bid-ask spread, but an unstable stock is more prone to manipulation and has a very big bid-ask spread. Stocks like AAPL, which trade in the $120 level, have a very narrow bid-ask spread-- typically a $0.10 difference between the Bid and Ask price. This is what I call a stable. There are other equities out there that are trading at $8 and with spreads of $7.10 and $9.15. Because of the large Bid-Ask spread, this is not a steady stock. It is ultimately up to you to determine what constitutes a "stable" stock.

After we've constructed our watch list, we'll set up our scan filters.

To scan for equities when a squeeze has triggered, enter the following code into ThinkOrSwim's Scan tab:

BollingerBandsSMA()."lowerband" >
KeltnerChannels()."lower_band" and
BollingerBandsSMA()."lowerband"
KeltnerChannels()."lower_band" and
BollingerBandsSMA()."lowerband"

A search using these criteria will reveal equities that have just launched a squeeze. As I often swing trade, I run this scan on a daily chart; however, the same code may be applied to a 1-minute or 5-minute aggregate period for day traders.

You may automatically monitor the markets for squeezes and successful trading opportunities by running this code via the monitor tab. It eliminates the need to repeatedly browse charts for an entry. You may use the following lines of code instead to search for stocks that are presently in a squeeze (red dots on the TTM Squeeze histogram):

BollingerBandsSMA()."Upperband" vs.
KeltnerChannels()."Upper_band" or
BollingerBandsSMA()."lowerband" vs.
KeltnerChannels()."lower_band"

ThinkOrSwim will provide a list of stocks that are still in a squeeze that hasn't yet fired off using this scan query. It is a great approach to locate stocks where you may enter a squeeze trade before it has really fired.

My next filter will check for a positive TTM Wave value in my scan query. This is because, given the present market circumstances, I am particularly searching for bullish squeeze trade opportunities. I use the following code to look for a positive TTM Wave:

def hist = TTMSqueeze.Histogram
def w1 = TTM_Wave.Wave1
def w2h = TTM_Wave.Wave2High

```
def w2l = TTM_Wave.Wave2Low
plot scan = w1 0 and w2h 0 and w2l 0
```

This code runs twice, once on a weekly and once on a daily timescale, to locate stocks that are in a squeeze, have a positive wave on the daily chart, and a positive wave on the weekly chart (our anchor chart). When finished, my filters in Thinkorswim look like this:

Trading at this phase consists of running your scan to locate trade setups for you to take, establishing effective price objectives using Elliott Lines, and then executing the trade.

When trading stocks, I have one more rule: I will never trade a company two weeks before or two weeks after it has disclosed profits or dividends. While this may seem unnecessarily cautious to others, I follow this guideline to prevent risk. Stocks may become exceedingly volatile during earnings season, to the point that even the strongest technical indicators fail.

CHAPTER 14

THE DAY AND THE SWING

Rather than investing in firms for long-term development, we will look at a short-term method utilized to generate income in the here and now. These techniques benefit by taking advantage of short-term swings in the stock price.

The two ways are as follows:

Trading throughout the day: Day trading is when you purchase and sell the same security on the same trading day. This is a tightly controlled activity. A brokerage will classify you as a day trader if you execute four-day transactions in any five-business-day period (this classifies you as a "Pattern Day Trader"). Most brokerages demand $25,000 in your account to be a day trader. A few businesses will allow you to day trade with tiny accounts, but they demand high charges. As a consequence, rookie day traders with little money utilize such firms to learn, while experienced traders use traditional brokerages to avoid the hefty costs.

Swing trading: is a less risky method. This is just a buy-low, sell-high approach that can go as long as you like, but only for a few months. Because a swing trader does not day trade, he or she will keep an investment for at least one night.

Swing trading is significantly lower risk because, unless the firm goes bankrupt or there is a massive recession (and presumably you are doing your homework so that you know what is possible), the stock is likely to go higher than what you bought for it in the near future.

Swing trading has no capital requirements due to its minimal risk.

Regardless of the variances, the methods remain the same. Day trading is a high-risk activity that is riskier than swing trading and considerably riskier than traditional stock investment. It's difficult to argue that swing trading is actually that risky when compared to purchasing shares of a single stock for any reason. If it is not lucrative to sell, the swing trader may just hold the stock.

Risks and Objectives

The purpose of day traders and swing traders is to profit in cash. As a result, rather than operating as an investment, consider it a trading company. You are more concerned with the company's short-term stock price volatility than with its long-term potential. The day trader is interested in benefitting from price variations that occur over the length of hours, minutes, and even seconds. A swing trader seeks to profit from price fluctuations in the share price that occur over a period of days, weeks, or even months.

One danger, particularly with day trading, is that emotion may take over.

This is true for both happy and negative emotions. As a result, you may have too much fear of loss and sell too soon, or you may get greedy and fail to sell when you should because you expect the share price to explode.

Another problem is that rookie traders do not apply typical risk-mitigation techniques that might reduce cash loss when their guesses go wrong. One issue is that many individuals just go on and start trading without understanding what is going on. Instead, you could invest in yourself by taking some day trading classes from specialists.

Profits that might be made

Most beginner-day traders will most likely lose money at first.

However, if you've put in the time to research and practice, including completing a course, you might be well on your way to being a great day trader. Those that are successful may earn large sums of money each year.

Risk Reduction Measures

Let's take a look at some crucial risk-mitigation actions you must take in order to effectively day trade without losing all of your money.

Specific Sell Criteria

If you want to benefit from a stock price increase, set a precise objective and sell when it hits the target. Assume you purchase shares of a certain stock for $10 per share and it begins to rise.

You have set a profit objective of $15 per share. When it reaches that level, you sell it and record your gains; you don't let emotion get the better of you and worry if it rises to $20 per share. A greedy or excessively enthused trader may hold the stock for too long, expecting it will continue to rise. However, it may suddenly go back to much lower levels than what they bought for it. When you acquire your shares, set a profit objective for yourself and adhere to it no matter what occurs.

Imposing a daily restriction

You may also protect yourself by setting a daily limit on how much wealth you're ready to risk each day. So maybe you limit yourself to buying $3,000 worth of shares (or whatever) to avoid risking the farm.

Margin trading should be avoided.

Many individuals fall into financial problems by using margin trading (borrowing money from the broker). You can avoid getting into difficulty in the first place if you don't spend what you don't have. Instead of getting emotional about some ostensibly "sure thing," have a steady plan for profits that you earn over time, rather than hoping that you've "found the big thing" and you're going to potentially get yourself into big trouble by borrowing a lot of money to realize your dreams when the odds are solid your predictions will be wrong.

Risk estimation

Let's have a look at how risk is calculated by advisers. The risk on a single transaction should be 1% of your account capital. Assume that shares of a certain stock are trading at $100 and you have $50,000 in your account. So, 1% of $50,000 is $500. That implies the maximum you can risk is $500, but that does not apply to the entire amount paid on the shares, so you do not purchase $500 worth of shares. That is, you place a stop-loss order to restrict your total loss to $500. So, putting a stop-loss order at $99 results in a $1 loss per share, allowing you to acquire 500 shares. So, you may put your whole $50,000 account in danger on the deal! However, with the stop-loss, if the price begins to fall, you'd immediately sell at $99 per share, giving you $49,500 at the end of the day. Assume it falls to $75 per share. It would have no effect on you if you used a stop-loss order. However, if you hadn't used a stop-loss order, you would have lost $12,500 on the deal.

Candles

When individuals' day or swing trade, they employ "technical analysis" to forecast the stock's future movements. The main distinction between the two trading techniques is the time periods used for analysis. A day trader would look at 5-minute intervals to decide what trades to make in the next few hours, while a swing trader might watch for huge fluctuations in stock price over the period of a few weeks.

Candles are one instrument utilized in the study. Candles may be shown on any stock chart by choosing them as a display option and setting the time length. Japanese rice merchants really created candles. Markets exist everywhere.

The candles have "wicks" protruding from them. These represent the time period's peak and low prices. Candles are either red or green. A red candle signifies that selling is dominating, while a green candle shows that purchasing is dominant. In other words, a red candle is related to falling stock prices, whereas a green candle is associated with increasing stock prices.

The top wick represents the period's highest share price. The bottom wick represents the period's low share price. What you choose for the chart settings determines the timeframe. So, on the chart with 5-minute intervals, the high and low prices represent the high and low prices for each 5-minute period.

The solid block is the body. If the block is green, the top of the body represents the closing price, and the bottom represents the initial price (price at the beginning of the time period). For a red candle, the top represents the beginning price and the bottom represents the closing price. So, a red candle shows that the price fell during the specified time period, whereas a green candle indicates that the price grew during the specified time period.

Candles are used by traders to estimate changes in the direction of the stock price. If a candle of one color engulfs the previous candle of the other color, indicating that its body is significantly greater in size, this might suggest that a price reversal is on the way. The photo above shows a red candle with a little body adjacent to a green candle with a very huge body, and the enormous green candle was followed by a rise in the share price. The huge green body shows that many individuals acquired shares of the company over that time period, and increasing demand suggests prices will rise. A hammer is a tiny candlestick with a long wick underneath it.

At the bottom of a downtrend, a green hammer might imply that stock prices are going to rise. As a result, that is a buy indication. If the hammer is turned upside down, it is known as an inverted hammer or, with a red candlestick, a shooting star. These occur near the apex of uptrends, indicating that the stock price is poised to fall. A shooting star indicates that it is time to sell.

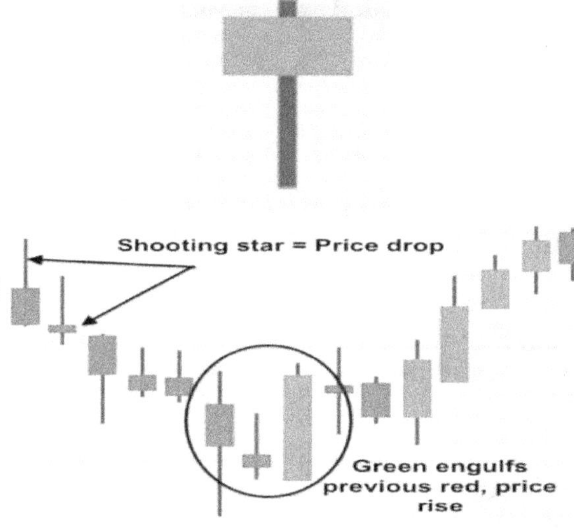

Day trading and swing trading are not for everyone, but they may be utilized to make quick money. Some individuals like stock research and are engaged in the stock's short-term movements, thus they take an active position in trading. If the concept appeals to you but day trading seems to be too hazardous, try swing trading, which isn't as risky in contrast, but you should always use stop-loss orders and be prepared to take gains when they come rather than holding too long in the hope of making additional profits. You may also vary things up by putting part of your money into long-term investments while using the rest to support some swing or day trading. People interested in short-term earnings in the stock market may also employ options trading, as we shall see later.

CHAPTER 15

HOW DO YOU BECOME A SUCCESSFUL DAY TRADER?

Before investing, you must have a goal in mind if you want to be a great day trader.

Making a Goal

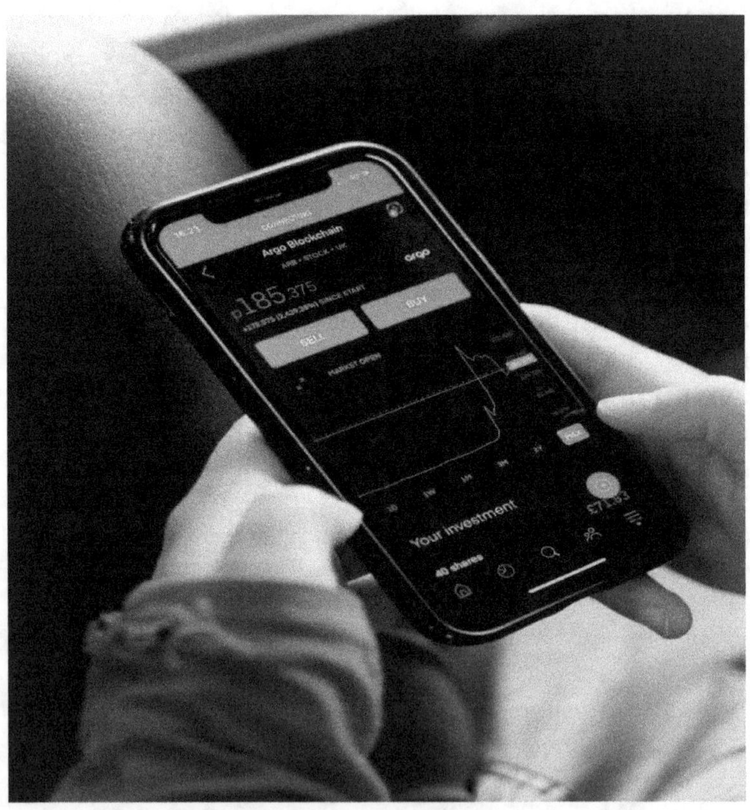

Define what motivates you to get out of bed and go to work every day. Do you want to go on vacation? Do you need to repay your student loans? Do you want to buy a new car? Whatever the reason, setting a goal will assist novice traders in reaching their full potential. A goal should always be quantifiable and tied to a timetable. Measurable objectives may show individuals how far they've gone, and timeframes enable them to fulfill deadlines and set new goals.It is critical to understand that day trading is not a "get-rich-quick" scam. Maintaining realistic objectives will aid in success.

Strategies

After you've defined your objective, the following stage is to plan how to make it a reality.It is critical to understand several principles that are directly related to your plan. These are the notions of necessary capital and leverage.

Leverage

Day traders may utilize their own funds (cash account) or borrow funds from a broker (margin account).This is a significant choice. Trading with a cash account is often a safer alternative, but gains are restricted to the amount of cash accessible to the trader.The most common among day traders are margin accounts. With a margin account, traders may utilize the broker's money to maximize profits per transaction, but they will also raise the amount they lose if the market falls.

Before enabling a trader to access the platform, brokers may additionally need a deposit into the account. With stocks, leverage is a simple idea. Assume a trader invests $1000 in XYZ Inc. by putting up $500 and borrowing the other half from the broker. The total value of the exchange is $1040. This means that the net equity is $540, and the trader received an 8% return on investment despite a 4% fluctuation in stock price. As a result of the leverage, the trader's returns doubled. However, this may have resulted in a loss that was twice as large.

How Much Should You Bet on Each Trade?

A lot in stock trading is typically 100 shares, and price increments are quite tiny. Assume a trader purchases a lot at $20 per share with a stop-loss of $19.50. The risk in this situation is $0.50.The total amount at risk for 100 shares is $50.Is this a good transaction to make? Most traders advocate keeping the acceptable risk at or below 1%. Regardless matter how wonderful the opportunity is, a trader should retain at least 99% of his or her account balance intact.

Let's apply this reasoning to the preceding situation. We are betting a total of $50, with a total account balance of $2000. We may calculate the balance of our account by dividing $2000 by 1%. The division offers us $20, which is 2.5 times the risk of $50. As a result, the risk associated with making this deal is much more than what we should risk each trade. According to the risk strategy, we need at least $5000 in the account balance to execute this transaction (which corresponds to a risk tolerance of $50).

Stock Picking

Successful day traders usually trade companies that have the most liquidity (traded in large quantities). One of the benefits of investing in a liquid stock is that it is simple to buy and sell. This is due to the vast number of shares available for trading without fear of substantial price fluctuations. Day traders must use speed and accuracy in their techniques while trading throughout the day. Day traders will find it simpler to initiate and exit deals when working with a high-volume stock.

Day traders must also consider market depth (the number of shares available for trading). This will inform them how many shares of a certain firm they may purchase without generating considerable price appreciation.Stocks with medium to high volatility are also popular among day traders. Price fluctuation is critical for day traders since here is where they may profit. As a result, selecting volatile stocks is critical. Volatile stocks are ones that have big price fluctuations, resulting in a considerable gap between their intraday high and low marks.

A day trader selects equities that are part of a group. What exactly are group followers? These are stocks or shares that mimic the fluctuations of their respective sectors or index groupings. How can you locate these stocks? Simple. Just look at how many individual stock prices rise as the index or sector rises. Take notice that if your approach is to trade the same stock every day, it doesn't matter whether the stock is a group follower. The best thing you can do is concentrate your efforts just on that one stock.

Only focus on the current intraday trend. If you've been around other traders, you may have heard the smart advice to "trade with the trend." The most seasoned traders will tell you to "trade with the trend" because "the trend is the day trader's best friend."But, as a trader, you must also understand that the trend will come to an end... and when that time comes, you must part ways. However, as long as the trend exists, you must ride the waves.

How do you go about it? Keep things simple, then.
Take long positions if you see an upward trend. As previously said, trends will not last forever, but you may make one or two trades before the trend changes. If you're fortunate, you may even be able to earn more. However, once the prevailing tendency changes, leave and do not return until a new trend can be noticed.
If you want to find the top stocks for intraday trading, compare them to the S& P 500 or Nasdaq indices. Look for stocks having a moderate to the high association with these indices. What kind of equities should you trade during an uptrend?

The Strategy for Entry
Always wait for the downturn; often traders get too eager, particularly during an uptrend, and opt to take a different path. But this should not be the case if you want to maximize your revenues. According to experts, waiting for a pullback would provide you with several rewards. How will you approach this?

Begin by examining the trend lines to get an idea of where the price waves will begin and terminate. You may use this while selecting stocks for trading to see if you can enter the following price wave early on, taking you in the direction of the trend. If you want to purchase a stock that is projected to gain in value, do it when you see a downward movement in the price and progress toward a higher point.

Profits should be taken on a regular basis. As a trader, you do not have a lot of time to capture gains, which is why it is critical that you do not waste time on trades that do not allow you to generate money. Also, avoid entering into transactions that are not heading in the proper way. When will you be able to profit? When the market is trending higher, you may take gains when the price meets or slightly exceeds the current trend's price high.

Stop-loss

Your safety net is a stop-loss order. It is the stock price level at which you will instruct your broker to automatically quit the deal and sell the stocks you purchased. This aids in limiting your losses. The amount of the stop-loss is determined by your risk tolerance and a technical study of the trend.

The relationship between your entry point and stop-loss is critical to comprehend here. The stop-loss is not static, but after you make the trade, you may adjust it based on the behavior of the trade, but remember that you can only change it in the up direction, never below the level you stated when you choose your entry point.

The Plan of Exit

If there is a point of entrance into trading, there must also be a point of departure. If you've been trading for some time, you'll know that getting into a transaction is far simpler than getting out of one. When you exit a deal, you will know if you earned a profit or suffered a loss.

A profit objective is the simplest approach to end or exits a deal.

A profit goal, according to Investopedia, is a "predetermined point at which an investor will exit a trade in a profitable position." Let's say your profit objective is $11.35. You purchased the stock for $11.25 and sold it for $11.35. When the price hits $11.35, you may close the deal.

Now, keep in mind that setting a profit aim must also be balanced. The key aim here is to maximize your earning potential based on the market trends in which you are trading.

If you are excessively greedy and set a high price, you may not attain your goal. If you place it too near, you could not make much money for your efforts. So, depending on your trading abilities, you must make a decision. One advantage of utilizing profit objectives is that you already know the risks and benefits of the transaction before you enter it.

Another advantage is that basing your profit goal on objective analysis can help you avoid trading emotions such as availability bias, loss aversion, and lottery syndrome.

This is because you already know your profit objective is in a favorable spot since it is based on the chart being reviewed.

One disadvantage of adopting profit objectives is that it requires a high level of expertise. You can't just throw them together at random. So, if you believe you are not talented enough in this method, consider alternative options or, better yet, improve your skills.

Another disadvantage is that it is always possible that your profit objective may not be met. This is bad because if you continue to set your profit objectives excessively high, you will lose all of your transactions. Similarly, if your profit objective is set too low, you will not benefit from taking risks. Fortunately, there are a few techniques for making the most of your profit objectives.

CHAPTER 16

CHOOSING THE BEST TRADING PERIOD

Whether you are a novice or a seasoned trader, you must begin depending on consistency. This will make it simpler for you to choose the correct companies to invest in and will help you determine whether or not you will earn a profit. A stock with continuous ups and downs in the market, for example, will be much simpler to invest in since you know when the high and low points will occur. A stock that is very volatile and without any pattern might be difficult to invest in since you never know where it will go from one day to the next. There are a few pointers you can use to help you decide when is the optimum moment to trade.

When trading stocks, the optimal times to do so are the first two hours after your chosen market opens, and again in the last hours before closing. So, trading between 9:30 and 11:30 a.m. is an excellent time to get started. This is an extremely volatile period, with many price swings and many opportunities to benefit. Then, try trading between three and four o'clock in the afternoon, since large fluctuations may occur during these periods as well. The morning session is the ideal alternative for traders who cannot trade all day and just have a few hours available.

If you want to trade futures, the optimum time to do it is when the market opens. Because active futures are always trading, the finest possibilities for this will frequently begin before the stock market starts. Try to concentrate your efforts on trading between 8:30 and 11:00 a.m. The official timing for shutting the futures market varies, but you may also look at trading in the last hour.

During the week, the currency market is open for business all day. EUR/USD is the most popular day trading pair that you may desire to trade with. The currency market is most volatile between six and five o'clock GMT. A day trader who wishes to deal with the forex market should devote the majority of his or her attention to trading during that period. Prices often fluctuate the most between 12 and 3 p.m. GMT. This is the period when both the US and London markets are open, which implies that both groups are trading heavily at the same time. Despite popular opinion, you do not have to spend all day on the computer performing your trades unless you want to.

This may be difficult to maintain and can lead to a lot of tension and stress. Many traders will be more consistent and generate greater profits if they simply spend a few hours trading in the market each day. Using some of the periods stated above, depending on the market you wish to trade in, may make a significant impact. Overall, you can make money trading at any time of day as long as you have a sound trading technique and know when to enter and leave the market. So, if there is any reason why you cannot be accessible at the start or finish of the market, don't worry too much about it. You may always trade when it is convenient for you.

CHAPTER 17

OPTIONS

Trading options is not a new concept in the world of finance. In truth, the practice has been prevalent since before 332 BC, since it was referenced in Aristotle's book Politics, which was published in 332 BC. This method permitted anyone to acquire the right to buy an item without actually purchasing the asset.

Aristotle introduced this subject by writing about Thales of Miletus. Thales was an ancient Greek astronomer, philosopher, and mathematician. His options trading career began when he utilized the stars and weather patterns to anticipate a massive olive crop the next year. Following his original forecast, he predicted that olive presses would be in great demand to handle such a massive crop. Thales, ever the visionary, realized that if he owned all of the olive presses in the area, he might make a fortune.

While he did not have enough money to purchase all of the olives presses altogether, he did utilize the modest cash he did have to acquire the usage of all of the olive presses in that area by utilizing the olive presses themselves as the underlying asset to execute the deal.
His forecast came true, and the olive crop was abundant. Thales had the choice to utilize all of the olive presses in the area at harvest season (exercising the option) or sell them to other persons who would pay more for the identical right that he had at the time (selling the options to make a profit). He elected to sell the privilege to use the olive presses to harvesters, making a tidy profit.

Options trading made its way into contemporary trading techniques in 1636, when it was introduced into European classic economics and finance. Options trading has a poor image as a result of uncontrolled operations.

However, this did not prevent investors from seeing that trading options provided them with significant financial leverage. Russell Sage, an American businessman, introduced options trading to the United States in 1872. Sage was able to amass millions of dollars via options trading in only a few years, despite the fact that the technique of trading options was illiquid and unstandardized at the time. In 1874, he even purchased a seat on the NYSE. Unfortunately, Sage lost a modest sum after the 1884 stock market fall and abandoned his trading choices. However, other traders and investors saw the potential of options trading and continued to use it.

It took roughly 100 years, but as options trading gained popularity, the government standardized and controlled it and additional breakthroughs were made in defining how the public traded options. I will be eternally glad that the approach withstood the test of time and become an essential component of current stock marketing investment.

My first foray into the stock market was via options trading. When I didn't have the funds to purchase and sell shares directly, options trading permitted me to access the stock market. Even though the learning curve was steep, especially since information was not as readily available when I first started, the benefits allowed me to accumulate enough wealth to turn to invest in more expensive forms of stock market trading such as buying and selling stocks, mutual funds, and exchange-traded funds.

Even though the price was reasonable, it was the no-obligation character of this kind of dealing that drew me in the most.

By trading options, I was under no legal obligation to acquire or sell anything until it was beneficial to do so. As a guy who did not have as many assets in his name when I first began trading, this was fantastic since the dangers were substantially smaller than the act of simply purchasing and selling stocks.

Because of the significant leverage trading choices available to me, I continue to employ this trading method to keep my portfolio balanced and to join markets that I am uncertain about but want to test for profitability. The nice thing is that getting started with options trading isn't all that different from getting started with stock trading. Make sure this technique is included in your trading strategy, that you have the proper accounts and representation via a brokerage business, that you get your feet wet with paper trading, and that you pick your trading style before you begin trading options. Day trading is the full-time activity of trading stocks and positions on the stock market. It is the most frequent stock market trading method utilized by experts. It is also the most popular options trading technique.

What are your options?
Stocks and options are often confused and misunderstood, but they are not the same thing. Stocks are a common component of options. Options are an excellent method to invest in the stock market without purchasing shares or any other investment altogether. This type of investing enables individuals to invest in the stock market with less money while yet having the opportunity to achieve the same return as a stock trader.

Options are financial contracts that receive their value from the securities to which they are linked. The contract says that the holder of the option has the right (option) to purchase or sell the securities at a set price on or before a defined date. The given date is known as the expiry date. The word option refers to the fact that the contract holder is under no obligation to perform any certain action.

The option holder's alternatives include:

- Selling the option to another investor.
- Purchase the asset under the terms of the contract.
- Use the option to sell all or a portion of the asset.
- Allow the choice to lapse without taking any specific action.

The striking price is the particular selling or purchasing price at which the option may be exercised. This pricing will not change regardless of what occurs after the signing date.

Instead of purchasing or selling the securities, options investors pay a premium to the option seller. Because there are so many aspects that go into producing each one, option premium pricing is a complicated process. It would be a straightforward procedure if the premium was only determined by the value of the stock or other securities, but this is not the case. There is no getting around the procedure since premium pricing must be fair to all parties participating in the transaction.

The intrinsic value of the security also influences the evolution of the option premium. This value is calculated by subtracting the current market price of the security from the strike price of the option.

Another aspect that contributes to an option's premium is its time value. Time value is the amount an investor is ready to pay in addition to the premium because they believe the security's value will grow in the future. Other elements that influence option premium formation include:

- Volatility
- Rates of interest
- Dividends

Fortunately, there exist pricing models that assist in the production of option premiums, eliminating the need to compute them manually.

CHAPTER 18

OPTIONS TRADING

Position trading is the practice of holding stock for many weeks or even months. Position traders hold positions for a longer length of time than swing traders. You are more focused on a long-term game plan, and you are convinced that the profits you will get with such a prolonged timetable will be greater than if you attempted alternative techniques. The three most important aspects of position trading are news trends, earnings cycles, and industry trends.

Trends in News
Traders that use a position trading technique invest in the stock. The fact that they're digging in for up to many months demonstrates that they're betting on the stock's value increasing as the market does.

The news surrounding the specific stock is one of the primary criteria on which they build their technique. Perhaps there is some kind of medicine application approval that is spending. Perhaps there is a new patent or program that has been introduced. Whatever the situation may be, there is an event that has been made public, and there is some type of deadline in the future for a decision on that event.

For example, a biotechnology firm may have been working on a game-changing cancer medication for many years. During that period, the stock may have gone up and down or traded sideways. A position trader would buy that stock if there was news that the FDA will make a decision on its medication application within the next few weeks or months.

Many biotechnology companies are pretty predictable in terms of their news cycles, which makes them attractive position plays. In order for a novel treatment to be authorized by the FDA in the United States, the drug application must go through many stages. There are three types of trials: lab trials, clinical trials, and official applications. Each of these news occurrences might represent a period in time when a position trader can invest in the firm.

To return to the biotechnology example, if a corporation is developing an anti-cancer medicine, it would first disclose that its lab findings show that they have a potential molecule. When the news breaks, it might be a good time to buy. However, it's anyone's guess if this potentially promising technology will ever be commercialized since the medicine must still go through internal laboratory testing, broader lab testing, human clinical trials, and official application.

A position trader may buy the stock and hold it till the next phase arrives. Typically, they would wait until clinical studies looked promising enough for the corporation to make a formal application. Once the business submits a formal application, the stock might move quite a bit.

Can you picture how the stock would react when the FDA ultimately approves the application? So, the crucial issue here is that for a biotechnology company's proposed medicine to be authorized, there are rather well-defined milestones. Position traders may use the milestones to plan their positions. It's very unusual for biotechnology stock traders to enter and exit a biotech stock numerous times as the firm gets closer to medication approval.

Strategic collaborations are another news trend to keep an eye on. For example, a corporation has just collaborated with a huge retail or pharmaceutical chain that operates throughout the United States. Such transactions and commercial advancements may have a significant beneficial influence on a company's sales results.

The position trader would then review the announcement and decide whether or not to invest in the firm based on the estimated timing for the revelation of the outcomes of that static partnership. Depending on the size of the transaction, the position trader may earn a lot of money if the distribution arrangement of the business alliance has a major influence on the company's bottom line.

The Earnings Cycle
Another relatively predictable milestone or combination of events allows traders to profit from our earnings cycles. A position trader would look at previous news releases to determine if there is a good or negative trend here when a firm is ready to declare its profits in a month. In any case, the position trader would open a position.

The position trader would purchase long in the event of a good trend. In the case of a downward trend, the trader would sell short. Whatever the situation, there is a very short and predictable period of time between when the trader opened a position and when the event of the profits occurs. Whether the corporation earned more or less money, the event will occur, and the position trader will be able to liquidate his or her position.

It's vital to notice that there is some difficulty. Wall Street has grown to the point that even if a firm meets expectations, it may not be enough to enhance the stock price. In many situations, Wall Street expects firms to outperform their peers in order to get a significant boost.

For example, if Facebook declared that it would be making a dollar per share and it really makes a dollar per share, chances are that performance has already been built into Facebook's stock price by the time its next earnings cycle milestone comes around.

Compare this to Facebook's announcement of a $1.25 profit per share. Assuming the consensus estimate was $1 per share, this is fantastic news. A position trader who purchased before the earnings cycle stands to make a lot of money if the firm beats expectations. When it comes to the earnings cycle, never underestimate the strength of street expectations.

Don't be startled if you buy a long position many weeks before the earnings cycle ends, only to see your stock stay the same or even fall in price. Keep an eye out for street expectations. It is not unusual for a firm to meet its declared earnings objective while yet seeing its stock price fall. Why? Wall Street expected the business to outperform forecasts. Simply showing up to satisfy expectations is insufficient.

If you think that's awful, wait till the corporation fails to meet expectations. If, for example, Amazon stock was projected to make $1 per share but instead earned 90 cents per share, the value may fall dramatically. Expectations should always be considered.

Trends in the Industry

Another important component in position trading is industry trends. If you observe that the industry as a whole is about to explode, you may invest in prominent firms in that field. It all relies on whether this sector's breakout or recovery is reflected in the stock prices of the largest firms in that industry.

The secret to playing industry trends is to avoid buying the industry's titans. Because everyone is paying attention to such firms, whatever acknowledgment you get is likely to be very incremental. Many individuals are betting on such firms. Any upward rise in your holdings would be diluted by the large number of persons purchasing and selling that stock.

Instead, search for mid-tier firms that have a history of doing well during industry recoveries. Alternatively, you might invest in growth stocks in that industry. The reason you should adopt this method is that the weight of return on your position will most likely be significantly bigger than if you bet on the top firms in the industry you're following.

You must recognize that the largest companies in any sector are generally already invested in by large mutual funds and pension funds. In summary, their institutional coverage is quite strong, thus they must significantly outperform the sector for their stocks to gain traction. This is not the case for middle-tier or emerging enterprises in that sector. If there is a good industry trend, the stock values of these firms may skyrocket.

Position Trading Risks
The main risk you incur when performing position trading is not that your stock will fall in value. Let's get it out of the way first. Even if your stock plummets, you should have a stop-limit order in place. That is, you determine for yourself going in how much you can afford to lose. You then place a sell-stop limit order at that price.

For example, suppose you invest $20 in stock. Then you decide on 10% as the most you're prepared to lose in that position. As a result, if the stock ever falls below $18, your position will be instantly neutralized. You will become bankrupt. You are entirely out of inventory. This is how you guard against your long position heading south.

This occurs all the time, believe me. It doesn't happen all the time, but it does happen, so you should be prepared. At the very least, you only lost 10%. You may then re-enter the market to recoup.Also, bear in mind that if you lose money in stock trading, you may use that loss to offset any future profits. Still, the main concern you'll have when using a position trading approach to stocks is that the equities won't move.

When you think about it, it may even be a good thing if the stock just drops. Because if it sinks, you've already put your stop-limit order, and you're out of that stock. It just did not work out. The worst thing that can happen is that the stock tracks sideways. For example, if you acquire a firm at $20 per share and hold it for a year, the price of the company will essentially range from $20 to $19 to $21, with little variation. What is the issue here?

The issue here is that your money is not increasing, thus you are not battling inflation. Second, you're spending a lot of money in terms of opportunity costs. Can you imagine if you had not invested in that company in the first place and instead traded another stock that is volatile enough to allow you to lock in a significant profit? Which position would you prefer?

You can guarantee that the opportunity cost of position trading is pretty high. This is why many position traders spread out their long holdings. They understand that certain stocks in a basket would fall, thus they will instantly liquidate their stake. Always keep an eye on your capital's turnover since the timeframe may be so long that it turns out it was not worth your time or work to invest in that company at all.

While the stock may gain a few percentage points here and there, you're hoping for a reasonably big return to completely recuperate and make up for any opportunity costs you may have incurred.

This is the secret to successful position trading. Make certain that the profit you received pays for or exceeds the period you waited for the stock to appreciate.

Scalping traders are classified into three types: swing traders, day traders, and scalpers. The three ways may be combined to form my favorite manner of operating.

Scalping is a phrase used to describe extremely short-term trading. Swing traders carry equities over to the following day, while day traders strive to extract as much value from the stock as possible in one day of trading. Swing and day traders both rely on technical analysis, with a dash of fundamental research thrown in for good measure.

Scalpers are entirely dependent on technical analysis. Their objective is to achieve anything in the near future. Changes of a few pennies for a few seconds to a few minutes are acceptable. This implies that scalpers must trade in higher sums than a day or swing traders in order to make a living from the market. Scalpers with little support (which, tragically, is the case for most of them) make up for their lack of funds by trading in financial instruments, which may be leveraged greater than traditional stock trading leverage. Futures, which may be leveraged twenty times more, options, and, of course, FOREX (foreign exchange), which can be leveraged up to 500 times more, represented as a 500:1 margin. The absurdity is that trading in these highly leveraged securities is more difficult and riskier than stock trading. Nonetheless, the promise of "getting rich quick" drives individuals with little money and no expertise into the most difficult regions of trading, where they often begin and nearly always finish their trading careers.

Scalping Methods

The first requirement is that you maintain your finger on the mouse and your gaze fixed on the screen. You must devote your complete attention to the stock. LIMIT orders must be used while buying and selling. You must not pursue the stock since scalping profits and losses are measured in a few pennies. In many circumstances, I put an evacuation order ahead of time. For example, if I purchase 3000 shares at $20 and expect a 30-cent gain, I will place a sell limit order on my trading platform for 1000 shares at 20.15 and 1000 shares at 20.25 And keep my finger on the mouse for the first hint of weakness so that I may sell the remaining 1000 shares.

Smart Money

Smart Money Scalps are intended to be short-term and so are not conducted in tiny numbers. Trading in modest amounts of shares leads to the "small-money syndrome" and failure.

Scalping is not done in tiny amounts of shares. New traders scalping in little amounts, such as 300 shares, are stuck in the trap of insignificant earnings, sometimes known as the "small-money syndrome." Selling 100 shares for a 15-cent profit seems to be too low a return, so they will attempt to draw the deal out for a few more cents, only to realize that they have delayed too long before selling. The stock drops by 10 cents, so selling is no longer worthwhile since the profit is much lower, and they wait a little longer. The stock then returns to its entry point, or even lower, and the scalping is over! In contrast, with huge numbers of shares, a good return is generated with each partial transaction locked in, without the need to deal with the small-money problem.

The Penny Scalp

Cent scalping is a trading strategy that aims to profit by one or a few cents on minor intraday changes in stocks with "locked prices." Stocks with locked prices have hundreds, if not thousands, of traders executing bids and requests at one cent above or below the stock's trading price. This is not a traditional trading strategy focused on noteworthy intraday movements caused by breakouts, breakdowns, or direction changes. Contrary to what we've learned so far, scalping for one penny is mostly motivated by a lack of volatility.

The Commission Barrier and One-Cent Scalping
The first need for using this approach is to have a big trading account. If you want to benefit from a one-cent change while avoiding the commission barrier, you must trade at least 10,000 shares. A profit of one penny on 10,000 shares is worth $100 after the commission is removed. The commissions using this strategy are the difference between success and failure.

Here's an illustration: Assume you earned one penny on 10,000 shares, resulting in a profit of $100. Assume you paid a one-cent commission per share and purchased 10,000 shares. The fee cancels out the $100 profit, and when you sell, you lose another $100. A total of $100 was lost. Even if you paid a one-tenth of a penny fee totaling $20 for both buy and sell executions, you still gave the broker 20% of your earnings.

This may seem acceptable to you, but keep in mind that when you lose (at least 30% of your executions will be losses), the loss plus the fee will equal $120. The weighted average is obviously working against you.

The solution is to ask your broker to define a different commission system based on the Per Trade Commission Plan rather than the Per Share Commission Plan because charging one cent per share is only worthwhile if you trade in quantities of up to 2000 shares per click.

If you trade in huge quantities, you will most likely be able to close on a price of $3 to $6 every click of the button, infinite in number.

Commissions are generally received rather than paid by large-scale dealers. How? When you place a bid and ask for orders and wait for them to be filled, you are increasing market liquidity! As we have previously learned, the ECN pays you a fee of $2 per 1000 shares when you do this. With a simple calculation, you can see that the relatively modest amount of 10,000 shares will result in an ECN return of 0.2 cents per share, or $20, while you only invested $6. What would happen if 100,000 shares were issued? The ECN return is valued at $200, but the commission remains at $6. Can you see where I'm heading with this? I know traders that make a fortune by purchasing and selling a share at the exact same price, earning hundreds of dollars from the ECN return alone. If they're fortunate, they'll also make another penny per share. Does that seem simple? No, it is not simple!

The Method of One-Cent Scalping Finds a low-cost stock first.
This should ideally be between $5 and $10, with minimal volatility and a daily volume of tens of millions of shares. The candidates alter depending on market activity, volatility, and price. Keep in mind that volatility is this method's biggest enemy. Consider how much money you might lose if the stock moved 10 cents against you! This is also why you MUST follow the following guidelines:

1. The stock must be going sideways with no discernible trend, or, in industry parlance, the stock must have a fixed price.
2. The stock must be free of volatility and fluctuate no more than 5-10 cents every day.

3. The market is drifting sideways with no discernible trend (this usually happens at lunchtime).
4. The stock may be purchased for up to $10. Even if your name is not Warren Buffet, you can purchase inexpensive stocks in huge amounts.
5. The stock has a high trading volume of tens of millions of dollars each day.

The easiest method is to choose a stock from the list that always includes the "top ten" high-volume equities traded on NASDAQ or NYSE. It is important to note that I am not referring to stocks that were on the list by luck, but to those that appear on the list on a regular basis. On certain days, you can choose Bank of America (BAC), Intel (INTC), Microsoft (MSFT), or another company. Citigroup (C) was formerly the scalpers' favorite since its price lingered around $4 in quantities of hundreds of millions of shares each day before the reverse split, as previously explained.

When you put these equities up on your screen, you will observe intraday volumes in the tens of millions, if not hundreds of millions, of shares, as well as a massive number of bids and askers. Many of them are engaged in the one-cent game.

Who moves the stock if no one wants it to move more than one cent? Of course, these would not be scalpers operating at the penny level, since they are effectively locking down the price and limiting change. The real change comes from the public and funds bidding and asking with long-term investment in mind, and they aren't concerned with whether the stock has increased or decreased by one cent.

Assume you've picked your stock and are ready to trade. The process itself is pretty easy but needs considerable skill. First, even if the price is going sideways, consider the general market trend as well as the trajectory of the stock. If the trend is up, you should go long rather than short, and vice versa. Now you must put your purchase limit order in the BID and patiently wait for sellers to meet your bid. After purchasing the necessary amount, you place a sell limit order on the ASK side with a profit objective of 1 to 3 cents and wait for buyers to reach your ask in the opposite direction.

There is no need to utilize the short order since the standard SELL will function just as a short on most trading platforms. Now that you have successfully sold the amount you purchased and added a double quantity to that sale, you are in a short and must position a double quantity on the BID side with a profit objective of 1 to 3 cents, repeating the cycle. When the market gets more turbulent, and you believe you are on the right side of the market direction, you should cancel the exit order and attempt to benefit from a few pennies more than the initial profit objective.

I'd want to emphasize once again that this approach seems to be straightforward. In actuality, it requires a great lot of patience, self-discipline, and intimate knowledge of the market. You must monitor the stock chart in one-minute candles. You should also keep an eye on the market chart, which will tell you if you should leave the trade with an unexpected loss or cancel an exit order and allow the market to carry you to surprise winnings of a few pennies.

CHAPTER 19

VALUE INVESTIGATION

The Warren Buffett School of Investment is another name for value investment or basic investing. Warren Buffett is a well-known investor across the globe. He resides in Omaha, Nebraska, and he is responsible for multiplying his investors' money thousands of times. I'm not talking about his investments being worth a few thousand dollars; I'm talking about thousands of percent gains. That's how great an investor Warren Buffet is.

The noteworthy part about his investment technique is that he pays no regard to the company's current pricing. Instead, he considers long-term worth. A company's stock may seem to be appropriately valued by today's standards. According to Buffett, the stock is really undervalued in terms of its potential worth.

Future value is the key to value investing. You'd have to look at the company's track record, present operations, and health, as well as the health of the industry it's in.
You then project this knowledge into the future while taking into account probable future situations. You buy in once you have a reasonably clear image, and it's vital to highlight that you don't leave. That is the whole purpose of value investing.

Your purchase and hold. You're in it for the long haul. This method is only for long-term investors. You may be wondering, "Well if I buy long, will I suffer opportunity cost because I could have made more money in the short term by buying a more volatile stock?"

Believe me when I say that biotech and internet stocks may be highly volatile. It is not unusual for traders to profit hundreds of dollars every day due to the volatility of these equities. They move so swiftly. Warren Buffett is unconcerned about any of this. Instead, his strategy is to keep the firm for many years, if not decades, until the stock has split several times or increased in value significantly.

If you ever need evidence of this, go no further than his primary investment entity, Berkshire Hathaway. Can you imagine if you had purchased Berkshire Hathaway in the 1980s? You'd be a billionaire today several times over. That is how great an investor Warren Buffet is. He believes in the long game. He believes in long-term investment.

Now, value investing may not be a good match for your financial objectives. If your immediate objective is to increase your money by 10% or 15% each year, value investing may not be a sure thing. You must realize that value investment considers growth over time. It might be a significant increase. We're talking about the company's stock price doubling or tripling, but when that will happen is anyone's estimate.

It's not unusual for a stock to gain 5% the next year, then 20% the following year, then 10% the following year, and so on. When you average everything out, the stock's price has really doubled, tripled, or even quadrupled.

How to Invest in Value
Warren Buffett is renowned for just perusing a company's financial statements and financial paperwork in the comfort of his office. He would then make phone calls to acquire million-dollar stocks. He just does that. He hardly seldom visits the real firm. He

hardly ever reads the newspaper or keeps up with corporate news.

He is just concerned about their numbers. I don't expect you to be so skilled at the game that you merely need to see numbers. This is why you must consider the following variables.

Concentrate on CASH FLOW.
Solid businesses have cash flow quantities that support their asking price. The firm must be making money. Even if it is not making a profit, it must have enough cash flow to support its price today or in the future. Cash flow is calculated by either P/E or price-to-book, depending on how speculative the company is.

(P/E) Earnings to Price: The earnings per share of the corporation are compared to the current stock price. For instance, if a corporation earns $1 per share and trades for $20 per share, its P/E ratio is 20. This represents the cash flow value in relation to the current price. If you're going to utilize P/E as your cash flow component, compare equities with similar fundamentals (industry positioning, book value, growth factors, and so on).

The cost of booking Ratio: After reviewing a company's balance sheet, you will be aware of all of its assets. Whatever amount remains after adequate depreciation and discounting is the liquidation value of the company's assets. In other words, if you were to liquidate the firm and get cash for all assets while paying off all debt, what would be left is the book value. The price-to-book ratio is the number of times the company's book value is multiplied to obtain its current per-share value. For example, if a corporation has a book value of $10 per share and trades at $100 per share, the price-to-book value ratio is 10.

Please keep in mind that there are other additional cash flow-based value calculation methodologies, but P/E and price to book are the most prevalent and should be sufficient to assist any novice investor. As you gain experience in trading, you may wish to experiment with other techniques of measuring cash flow.

Concentrate on Industry Leaders

The first step is to hunt for industry leaders or future leaders in a certain area. It is critical to look at reputable businesses. These businesses are doing something right. They are profitable. They have created an impression. They have their act together. It is critical to concentrate on these characteristics.

The issue with a lot of stock out there is that it is sold based on enthusiasm and promise. Twitter, for example, has gone as high as the mid-40s because investors believe it will generate money someday. Its value was not dependent on how the firm was handled, how much money it made, or its industry position. It makes no difference. The whole emphasis was on prospective expansion.

This is not the case with value investment. You consider the company's current status and the fact that it is already profitable. You begin with that reality. The firm must already be well-positioned. This does not imply that the corporation has already dominated or is the dominant player in its industry. It may be a rising star. What matters is that the home is in order.

It had to have financial stability

The absence of debt is a vital signal that a company's financial house is in order. A corporation with absolutely no debt and a low stock price is genuinely undervalued. This is the kind of combo that Warren Buffett is enthusiastic about. He is well aware that, for one reason or another, the market is simply not recognizing a company's strong fundamentals. One important element is its debt exposure.

If a firm has nearly no debt, a cheap stock price, and a strong market or industry presence, it has a considerable possibility of being an excellent value investment. However, you must also consider other considerations.

The company operates in a developing industry.
Can you imagine performing stock research and discovering a firm that is either about to become an industry leader or is currently an industry leader with no debt? It is also highly lucrative right now.On top of that, its stock is relatively cheap, as assessed by the price-to-earnings ratio (P/E). Doesn't it sound like a slam dunk?

Hold your horses, then. Pay attention to the firm that is in that field. That firm may turn out to be the lone jewel in that sector, given that industry is essentially in decline. such a company's future is likely to be grim under such circumstances. Its stock price may seem to be high today, but it is only a matter of time before the firm implodes or is forced to reinvent itself and join a new industry.

Keep an eye on the industry. Is it experiencing significant disruption? Is it still a thriving industry? The difficulty with sectors that are undergoing significant change is that you never know where the industry will go.

Eastman Kodak Corporation, for example, was the industry leader in photography materials. The photographic material sector is a shell of its former self as a result of the introduction of digital cameras. It still exists in a very limited form, but it is clearly not large enough to support a firm the size of Eastman Kodak. Do you understand how this works? And the issue was that the industry had been severely disrupted throughout the 1990s and early 2000s.

Avoid firms that are undergoing disruption since it is anyone's guesses what the final path of the technology or business strategies of the companies in that area will be.

Large cash position and high cash flow
Another issue that value investors consider is how much cash a firm has on hand. This is the primary measure of how effectively the organization is managed. If a firm is successful but spends all of its leftover capital on R&D, the company may not be a good value investment since it is effectively spending a lot of money to earn a lot of money.

Ultimately, it's simply trying to stay afloat. This is not always true. It is also determined by the industry. Still, if a company has a lot of cash on its balance sheet and almost no debt, that company is doing something right, and if the cash on hand is growing over time, this is a key indicator that this company may be a solid value investment, all else being equal.

Pay close attention to your accounts receivable. While a respectable amount of accounts receivable is acceptable, a firm with an extraordinarily high A/R level warrants additional and deeper investigation. It may be having difficulty gathering, and you must be extremely cautious about how they record them. The corporation may just seem to be worth a lot of money.

"Underappreciated Stocks"
These are stocks that are undervalued.
Warren Buffett is a great fan of undervalued stocks. In fact, he often mentions purchasing undervalued stocks in his interviews. Many people now describe

"underappreciated stocks" as firms whose stock prices are low in comparison to other Dow Jones Industrial Average companies.

This is a misunderstanding. In traditional value investing principles, a company is underestimated not because of how it compares to other firms, but because of its potential future worth.

CHAPTER 20

INVESTING IN DIVIDENDS WHAT EXACTLY IS DIVIDEND INVESTING?

Dividend Investing is a phrase used to describe an investing strategy that comprises acquiring dividend-paying equities. The primary purpose of dividend investing is to generate consistent passive income. Dividend investing is more complicated than its term suggests. There are complexities involved.

This may make the book a little harder to grasp for individuals who are not in the financial area. However, here are some phrases to keep an eye out for when reading. Knowing these terminologies will make it easier to utilize them in the future. Stock: A kind of security that corresponds to proportional ownership in the issuing firm. A stock may also be referred to as a share.

Dividend: A dividend is simply a percentage of a company's earnings distributed to its shareholders. Dividends are not always paid in cash. They own stocks and other real estates.

If you are not yet persuaded by the benefits of dividend investing, it is time to reconsider. There are several advantages to dividend investing, but the most obvious one that everyone will appreciate is that it is an excellent source of retirement income. When you retire, you have the option of taking part in your dividend payments while still owning stocks that will continue to pay you for the rest of your life.

Why Should You Invest in Dividend Stocks?
Despite the economic relevance of dividend stocks, there are articles, publications, and even professional opinions that dismiss dividend investing. As a consequence, many consumers are unsure whether or not to invest in dividend stocks. "What if the company abruptly reduces the price of its dividends?"

"I read in an article that dividend payments do not affect share prices." These remarks are some of the reasons why some people are uncertain about investing in dividend stocks. Nothing in our life is without advantages and negatives. The same logic applies to dividend stock investments. The good thing about dividend stocks is that the benefits far outweigh the drawbacks.

Furthermore, the minor disadvantages of investing in dividend stocks should not deter you from pursuing a consistent income. If you want to earn money as an investor, you must be ready to take risks. Even if you decide not to invest in dividend stocks, you are taking a risk. You run the risk of not benefitting from dividend stock profits. Despite the minor drawbacks of dividend stocks, there are several reasons why you should invest in them. So, to answer the main question:

What Are the Advantages of Investing in Dividend Stocks?

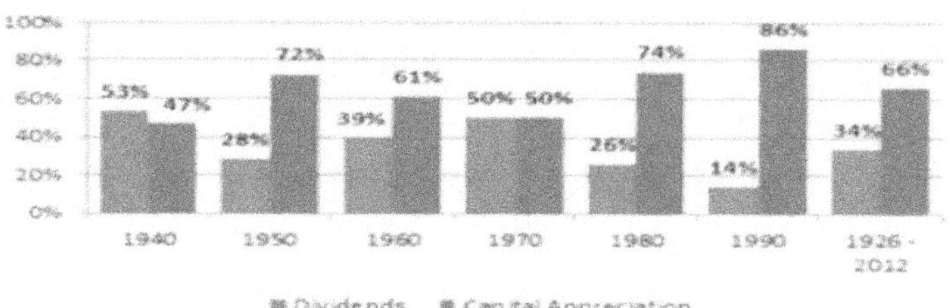

An illustration of how dividend investment may quadruple your gains over time.

Dividend stock investing may provide a steady stream of income.

One advantage of dividend stocks over other kinds of equities is that they provide a constant and predictable source of passive income. Unlike other types of investments, you do not need to sell anything to earn.

When you buy other sorts of stocks, you usually don't earn a profit until you sell them. The disadvantage of this trait is that you only have a paper profit until you sell anything. Yes, you earn money. However, the gain is just on paper since you cannot pay out your awards and profits until you sell anything. As a result, most assets are not suitable for generating a consistent passive income.

When you invest in dividend equities, the situation is different. The major difference between dividend stocks and other investing alternatives is that there are no paper earnings. When you invest in dividends, you have the security of receiving raw and cold cash. When it comes to dividend investing, there is no hard and fast rule about telling your broker to sell anything.

Dividends are money you earned. They cannot withdraw from you after you have been paid; this is the nicest thing about investing in dividend stocks. Furthermore, it is customary for corporations to pay dividends on a quarterly basis (that is, every three months). Dividend stocks are an investment choice to explore if you are an investor looking to multiply your income. There is a guarantee that you will be paid every three months. Say goodbye to financial insecurity.

Investing in dividend stocks yields a sufficient income throughout retirement.
When you invest in dividend stocks over time, you will have a steady income when you retire. Here's why you should start investing in dividend stocks as soon as possible.

According to research conducted by numerous financial specialists, investors who develop a dividend stock portfolio for the long term are more likely to purchase a large number of shares as they age. The consequence of owning a large number of dividend-paying equities in your retirement years is that you have more than enough money to cover your financial needs.

Dividend-paying equities are more likely to outperform their peers in the long run. When you purchase dividend-paying stocks, you are secure in your choice because you know you are making a financial move that will provide you with financial independence. Investing in dividend stocks provides both short-term and long-term benefits.

For example, by the age of 40, a nurse named Jane takes efforts to secure her financial future by investing in dividend stocks. If her dividend income is $50 at the moment, it will rise to $100 over time and continue to add up. Jane's dividend income would have piled up to $20,000 in equity by the time she reaches 60. Invest in dividend stocks if you want to be like Jane, or even better.

Investing in dividend stocks allows you to keep your shares and ownership at the same time.
Dividend stocks are not like other types of investments. Typically, if you buy from a company that does not pay a dividend, the only option to profit from your shares is to sell them. The idea is that you cannot earn a profit while still owning your shares. You cannot generate a profit while holding ordinary shares; you must offer something in exchange for something else.

Many individuals avoid investing because they are afraid of losing ownership in order to benefit. Because of their generalization of stocks, they are very cautious about any kind of investment. Not all stocks are created equal. Dividend stocks, for example, vary greatly from other forms of equities that do not pay dividends.
As humans, we are naturally greedy, and we dislike losing.

As a result, we are continually looking for methods to profit. We do not accommodate the dread of losing money, which is why some investors dislike the concept of selling shares. They believe that selling their shares in a firm will have an impact on them, particularly during times of expected growth. As a result, individuals tend to reject the concept of investing in stocks because they feel that making a profit means losing their source of income and ownership in a firm.

As previously said, not all stocks are created equal. The shares that do not produce dividends deny the twin privilege of ownership and profitability. Dividend-paying stocks allow you to profit from your shares while maintaining ownership. You do not have to worry about losing your ownership in a firm if you invest in dividend stocks. With a dividend stock investment, you earn from your equities while also holding them for the chance of financial gain.

Dividend stocks are largely unaffected by inflation.
During times of high inflation, your profits suffer. Despite the negative effects of inflation, you may protect your passive income from the harmful effects of inflation on the economy. You may WIN (Whip Inflation Now) by investing in dividend-paying equities.
If you are a history buff, you will recall that the WIN term originated during President Gerald Ford's administration.

If you're not sure what occurred, here's a brief rundown. In August 1974, President Ford encouraged Americans to Whip Inflation Now (WIN), citing the country's rising inflation rate (about 11%). And the WIN method was beneficial to most Americans because it offered a buffer against inflation.

Dividend stocks safeguard your investment returns from inflation, so they are a good choice if you want to be well-protected during inflationary times. Invest in dividend stocks if you want to grin while everyone else is crying wolf.

Dividends have a substantial advantage over other income-generating assets in that they can stay up with the rate of inflation.

Dividend stock prices rise in tandem with the overall price level of an economy. Companies make more money as prices rise. Companies' higher profits allow them to enhance dividend payout rates. As a result, you benefit more as an investor. However, inflation continues to eat away at your investment income, as a 3% increase in inflation might lower your 7% yearly gains to a measly 4%.

Investing in dividend stocks is a win-win situation.
Most investing solutions do not enable you to win completely. For example, if you exclusively invest in ordinary shares that do not pay dividends, you are likely to prosper in just one manner. The only way to win is to sell the shares for a high price.

Ironically, you incur a greater loss since volatility is nearly associated with Wall Street (the stock exchange market). There is no guarantee that share prices will rise to the point where you will benefit. Even though a period is steady, the stability is often fleeting owing to frequent variations in share value. As a result, when you invest in ordinary shares, you risk losing money in two ways.

Profitability drops at regular periods, and, more significantly, you lose control of your stocks. When you invest in dividend stocks, your position improves somewhat. While you are vulnerable to the same culture of Wall Street insecurity, investing in dividend companies gives you greater security. Dividends, unlike other forms of shares, provide a win-win situation. You have relatively steady ownership of your investments while earning money from them. If the issuing firm pays you a dividend and your stock value rise at the same time, you will gain a lot of money from both income and capital appreciation. If you don't want to get your dividend right away, you may reinvest it in additional equities.

As previously noted, Wall Street is not without its challenges. When you invest in dividend stocks, you might also lose money. Investing in dividend stocks does not protect you against frequent losses. However, you are safer than if you just invest in equities that do not provide dividends.

CHAPTER 21

INVESTING FOR GROWTH

Growth investment is sometimes compared with value investing as an entirely distinct approach to generating money in the markets. Both techniques, in fact, overlap with one another. This will provide you with a thorough overview of growth investing and explain how you may capture growth effectively and with as little risk as possible in your portfolio.

Definition

So, what exactly is growth investing, and why is it a desirable strategy to follow? As the name implies, the goal here is to capture a company's intrinsic development. The goal is to find firms with significant growth possibilities in the future and the profitability and competitive advantage to back them up. The goal of growth investing is to generate capital gains.

This is because organizations that are rapidly expanding need all of the capital, they can get their hands on. As a result, paying dividends may not be the best choice. Thus, investors who invest in growth companies are betting on the stock price growing enough to provide them with sufficient long-term benefits. This seems to be a dangerous method, yet that is exactly what smart investment entails.

After all, the goal of investing is to profit from a gain in stock price. Growth-oriented strategies simply take this a step further by requiring that a firm have a strong competitive advantage as well as a reasonable price value. This is where growth investment differs from value investing. The price of an investment is very important to value investors.

Assume there are two firms, A and B. Assume A is a mediocre firm that will not survive for more than ten years from now. B, on the other hand, is a fantastic firm with outstanding development possibilities. Currently, A is selling for around 65% of its value, but B is selling for 95% of its value, as calculated by an investor.

A value investor would normally choose A, whereas a growth investor would choose B. This highlights one of the most significant benefits of growth investment. By definition, it is intended to be a long-term approach. Companies do not expand overnight, and in order to get the full rewards of the techniques, you must remain involved for the long term. Let's look at some of the additional benefits of investing in this manner.

Excellent Corporations

Growth investment techniques put a high value on a company's ability to stay competitive over lengthy periods of time. Over time, a company's stock price mirrors its profit growth. As a result, in order for the price to rise, profits must rise at a similar rate. This is only possible if the firm has a substantial competitive advantage in the market and in its industry.

All of the large corporations you hear about now were originally growth-oriented. Apple, for example, was a model growth stock in 2002-2003. The firm was preparing to launch its next generation of devices, and Steve Jobs' vision for the company had just recently started to be realized. The corporation had a significant competitive edge in that it could charge any price it wanted for its items and consumers would still pay.

Customers were ready to wait in line for hours outside Apple shops for the gadgets. Any new Apple product was a significant event, and their goods quickly created whole side businesses, such as iPod and iPhone accessories. The fascinating part was that Apple stock was never cheap by normal measurements throughout this upward trip.

In comparison to its profits, the firm sold for a quite high multiple. The shares closed at $1.05.05 in 2003. The stock is now trading at $267.99. Remember, this is after many stock splits. In 2006, Apple announced a two-for-one stock split, followed by a seven-for-one stock split in 2014. This suggests that actual gains are much greater than the difference in stock prices between then and today.

Has Apple still considered a growth stock? Most likely not. It is the largest firm in the world, yet it seems to have exhausted its creative abilities when it comes to releasing game-changing items. This is not a terrible thing in and of itself. It is difficult for giant corporations like Apple to continue inventing and disrupting their sectors. It is significantly more advantageous for them to just retain and solidify their industry position.

My thesis is that the benefits of growth investment are enormous. Amazon, like Apple, was once a growth stock. Some may claim that it is still a growth stock. Microsoft, Walmart, IBM, Intel, and other companies were formerly considered growth stocks.

On the cutting edge
Growth investment firms often sustain their market edge over extended periods of time. This is because the sectors in which they operate are often at the forefront of change. Using Apple as an example, the technology sector has seen significant transformation since the turn of the century.

development investment allows you to capture not just business development, but also the benefit of being engaged in a whole sector. As a result, rather than just one stock gaining, a whole group of firms is rising. As additional investors invest in these equities, this tends to stimulate even greater growth. Along with Apple, stock prices for Google, Facebook, Amazon, and Netflix have skyrocketed.

Netflix is an excellent illustration of how the development of an entire industry can benefit a firm. Netflix began as a minor rival to Blockbuster's mail-order movie business. However, they quickly shifted to a streaming service before anybody had even heard of 2G. Many individuals did not comprehend the business concept, nor did they comprehend the magnitude of CEO Reed Hastings' goal.

Hastings' aim was to capitalize on the expansion of digital services and infrastructure in the latter several years of the previous decade to provide Netflix with a viable platform. Leaving aside the fact that the tech sector delivered on its promises, imagine a world in which tech businesses did not generate any buzz and Silicon Valley did not gradually replace Wall Street as the economic heart of America.

Netflix's prospects of success in such an atmosphere would have been exceedingly slim. Without the excitement generated by the growth of technology in general, no one would have paid close attention to the company's or its business model's rise. Netflix has numerous rivals now, yet it still has a significant position in the hearts and minds of those who use its services.

This merely goes to demonstrate that by adopting growth investing principles, you will not only discover one investment, but a whole universe of investments and businesses that will rise alongside it and take their position in the new economy.

Excitement

This one may seem paradoxical, but bear with me. Many investors find it difficult to adhere to long-term plans because they are tedious. For example, if you invest in individual firms that pay high dividends, you'll discover a lot of your money in utility stocks. Utility corporations aren't exactly lighting up the earth. They work in heavily regulated businesses with price caps.

They are solid investments with very predictable profits. Their stock prices will not fall much during weak markets, nor will they gain significantly during bull markets. In a nutshell, they're the ideal boring stock. Many investors will struggle to maintain their discipline and stick to these assets.

They will desire excitement since that is what the stock market's dominant message is. They'll hear their friends and neighbors discussing intriguing investments and want a piece of the action. As a consequence, they will abandon the long-term holdings norm and switch tactics.

Growth investment mitigates this to a considerable part since the firms you discover are in fascinating and cutting-edge fields. Their stock values will fluctuate. The degree to which the price changes in either direction is referred to as volatility. The prices of growth stocks tend to fluctuate a lot, which gives some fun.

The disadvantage is that if they go too much to the downside, investors may be forced to sell. However, if the company's decisions are correct and you follow the recommendations in this section, your loss will be minimal, making it unlikely that you would sell. Instead, you'll see the stock accomplishing something every day, which provides its own feeling of validation. As a result, you're far more likely to adhere to your plan and avoid undermining yourself by selling too soon.

CHAPTER 22

STOCK SELECTION STRATEGIES

To prosper in the stock market, you must master certain strategies. Maintain your adaptability: A stock market is a turbulent place, which means that if you ever intend to be successful in investing, you must be prepared to pivot at any time. The market may alter in a matter of minutes, which implies that a stock that has been profitable for a long time might suddenly flip around and become worthless, virtually overnight. This indicates that if you want to succeed, you must restrict the effect of the past on your actions and instead concentrate on the knowledge available in the present and what it will most likely signify for the future. If you want to achieve consistent long-term returns, you must be willing to abandon failing investments and rethink earlier decisions.

Commit to a strategy: The strategy you design will be important to your long-term success, but only if you adhere to it every time you make an investing decision. While it will not lead to success with every trade, if you design it using the appropriate criteria, it should lead to successful trades more than 50% of the time, which means you will succeed in the end if you stay with it faithfully. Furthermore, understanding the permissible criteria for selling and purchasing is critical to ensuring that you can capitalize on rising trends when they will benefit you the most.

Expectations have been measured: While it is possible to become wealthy by investing in the stock market, it is difficult since this kind of development does not occur immediately. Rather, most individuals who succeed there gradually accumulate assets over time by hanging on to winning investments and exiting those that don't turn out before they cause too much damage.

Furthermore, it is possible that it will take you a long time to get the hang of things, which means you can anticipate having a losing record for the first few months you start investing in stocks while learning the ropes. Keep in mind that this is normal; continue with it if you want to pass from red to black. Going into the process with a realistic notion of what it will take to succeed is an excellent method to ensure that the learning curve is as reasonable as feasible.

Select customized strategies: Just because you read about a method that is sure to work because someone else has achieved success with it does not mean it will work for you. While there is no reason not to give it a go, it is critical to ensure that it meets your own criteria as well as your natural investing inclinations. If it does not, the investment is unlikely to provide the desired effects. Instead, it is always crucial to be on the lookout for new tactics that align with your own preferences to utilize as a stepping stone to stock trading success rather than walls that must be overcome in order to see any returns. Being loyal to yourself will always be the most dependable method to see long-term beneficial outcomes.

Maintain discipline: Many beginning traders may pursue one sort of stock just because they have a gut feeling about it. The unfortunate reality is that gut instincts seldom, if ever, pay off efficiently. As a result, if you take this haphazard approach, you will make it more difficult to produce a profit in both the short and long run. Worse, if you do wind up succeeding with this technique, all you will have learned are undesirable habits, which will translate to fewer total achievements in the future. Instead of relying on your intuition, it is critical to concentrate on developing the discipline required to make the correct decisions, even if your stomach is telling you otherwise. While this may most likely be difficult at first, it will get easier with time.

Look for the exact truth: It makes no difference whether you believe a stock's price is too low or too high; the only thing you can consistently concentrate on is its present price. If the facts indicate that a stock's value should be greater than it is now, you should purchase; if it is lower, you should sell; end of the story. You must stay objective in the face of these realities and just follow their instructions. Getting too attached to a certain stock can only hamper your performance in the long term.

Concentrate on logic: Following your strategy perfectly with each deal you make will always be the most logical next step once you've developed a successful plan. This implies that even if the deal doesn't wind up working out as planned, you should be happy with yourself since you did what made the most sense at the time. Going off the book will almost always result in failure rather than success. Instead of being angry over lost transactions, consider them a statistical balance to the other more lucrative deals you're likely to make more than 50% of the time, providing your strategy is good.

Sometimes doing nothing is the best option: If you have cause to think a certain stock is overpriced, you should sell it; if it is undervalued, you should acquire it. When a stock is stopped in the middle of the road, the best course of action is to wait for a stronger signal to arise indicating a movement in one way or another. Waiting without making a move is one of the most difficult things for many beginning traders.

Making deals only to trade is usually a bad idea. When the market is stagnating or moving quickly, be patient. Wait till things settle down to reap consistent gains. Your objective should always be to make trades for profit, not merely to trade for the joy of trading.

Understand that there are no guarantees: the chances of discovering a system that successfully predicts trades 100% of the time, or even 90% of the time, are very slim. In reality, you have a higher chance of winning the lottery or being hit by lightning than of matching those numbers. Even before you include chance and plain, stupid luck, there are just too many factors to consider at all times. Rather than spending time seeking the unattainable, you will get much greater outcomes if you look for a strategy on which you can depend and accept any extra loss with a grain of salt.

CHAPTER 23

RISK MANAGEMENT

There are several sorts of risks in the stock market. Some are straightforward, such as a tiny business with the potential to profit from new items. Others are indirect or external in nature. You cannot handle every form of risk. Some occur unexpectedly, such as the 9/11 terrorist attacks or the 2008 financial meltdown. So, if you believe you can manage every kind of risk, take a big breath and admit you can't. We will attempt to detail every major type of risk that investors encounter, and if feasible, we will recommend solutions to cope with them.

Person and Emotional Risk

First and foremost, you have control over the dangers to your assets caused by personal circumstances. Fear, impatience, and greed are examples. Emotions like these might be difficult to regulate, but learning to control them is vital if you want to be a successful investor. When actual money is at stake, these feelings may become intense and overwhelming. You must not allow this to happen.

Fear is the most prevalent issue when it comes to emotions and personal danger. When the stock market begins to turn negative, many investors abandon ship. They are making a major error. A smart investor does not jump in and out of the market at the first indication of trouble. In fact, selling when everyone else is may be one of the most common blunders that individual investors make. Large investors, by the way, are not excluded. During downturns, many expert traders experience the same emotions and display the same behavior. Bear markets form as a result of massive sell-offs.

First and foremost, keep in mind that you want to hold your assets for the long term. So, market ups and downs, as well as recessions, are not reasons to sell them. The 2008 financial crisis was by far the greatest stock market downturn in the previous 50 years. Even so, it was only temporary. People who sold their assets had the choice of being out of the market entirely or returning to the market when prices were rising. Other significant bear markets had lifespans that were comparable or even shorter. The first lesson in personal risk management is to hold your assets during downturns.

The second lesson is that instead of succumbing to panic, you should begin to see market downturns as opportunities. You should purchase shares when prices are quickly falling owing to a market sell-off. It's hard to determine where the bottom of a market is, and you shouldn't worry about it. When share prices are falling, it is a buying opportunity, and you should make frequent stock purchases. On average, equities acquired during a slump will be worth much more than one year, two years, or five years later. Greed is the second issue that occurs as a result of personal danger. When individuals start investing, they often envision monetary signs.

A get-rich-quick mindset is incompatible with effective investment. Your strategy should be concentrated on gradually and consistently creating money rather than earning a fast profit. You'll come across promises that specific trades or stocks are the next best thing as you invest, but you're better off ignoring such statements.
They are often shown to be untrue. Even though many individuals regard the stock market as if it were a gambling casino, it is not.

You may avoid falling to greed by sticking to a regular investing plan and resisting the urge to benefit from short-term fluctuations or "penny stocks" that are expected to go off. Finally, there is the issue of impatience. Following the Great Depression, individuals acquired a more rational and conservative attitude toward the stock market. They learned that you won't get wealthy in six months or a year. The concept of long-term investment grew to dominate. Unfortunately, this lesson seems to be fading in recent years.

People are acting more like traders than investors. Far too many investors are seduced by the prospect of outperforming the market. Instead of being impatient, accept that you're in it for the long haul. You want to grow wealth rather than earn a few more dollars today.

Capital Loss Possibility
Obviously, financial risk is involved with investing.
Theoretically, you may lose all of your money if you invest in the stock market. This is possible if you bind your destiny to a limited number of corporations. Several well-known corporations, like Lumber Liquidators, Bear-Stearns, and GM, have either experienced serious troubles or gone bankrupt. Investors may have lost a lot of money in the process. The solution is to avoid investing in a limited number of firms.

You should also consider the sorts of businesses in which you invest. Investing your whole portfolio in small-cap companies, for example, is usually a terrible choice. Putting all of your money into developing markets or one area of the stock market is also risky. The essential lesson is once again diversity. It is a method of protecting yourself from financial danger.

Risks in the Market and the Economy

Some things are beyond your control, and the economy will always experience slowdowns and downturns. The market will cycle along with the economy, and it may fall even while the economy is doing well overall.

Political Uncertainty and Government

Government and politics may pose significant threats to the stock market. Market collapses may be caused by international events, and these days, even a tweet from the President can influence markets to rise and fall. Some lawmakers have recently discussed splitting up the large tech giants. Others are considering looking into them. Such words, and even worse deeds, may have a detrimental influence on markets. As an investor, you must keep a constant watch on the news. You'll want to know what's going on so you can make adjustments as needed.

Risk of Inflation

Inflation has not been this low for decades. In the late 1970s, however, inflation rates were consistently in the double digits. Hopefully, it will not happen very soon, since excessive inflation rates may eat away at your gains. If the stock market grows at 7% per year and inflation is at 14%, it's clear that holding debt while investing in equities is a losing proposition.

Inflation risk is now quite low, but you should be aware of it and keep an eye on it at all times. High inflation rates are also associated with high-interest rates since the Federal Reserve will hike rates to attempt to decrease inflation. This implies that bonds may become more appealing if inflation becomes uncontrollable.

Risk versus Return

A risk vs. return trade-off is one of the most basic decisions that an investor will make. In general, the larger the risk, the greater the prospect of excellent rewards. Amazon was a high-risk investment in 1998.

While it had promise, the sector was dominated by large booksellers such as Borders and Barnes & Noble. Amazon was on a fragile foundation at the time, and another business might have successfully competed for online book sales. That never occurred, and Amazon went on to dominate book sales while also expanding into retail and cloud computing. This risk has resulted in enormous profits. A $10,000 investment in 1998 is now worth more than $1 million.

However, hindsight is 20/20. Today, there are comparable changes all around us, but it's difficult to predict which ones will be successful in the long run. If you are an active investor, determining which firms are the greatest chances for the future will be part of your job.

Risk versus return is especially important in developing markets. Because they have so much opportunity to develop, these nations may enjoy tremendous GDP growth year after year. Domestic enterprises that expand in tandem with their economies may provide extraordinary rewards. However, there are several dangers. Rapid development is often accompanied by severe downturns. Emerging markets have less stability; you might lose all of your money. These examples demonstrate the importance of having a diverse portfolio.

Risk Administration
There are a few time-tested risk-management solutions that have been created. They even limit, to the greatest extent feasible, the types of danger that you will confront that are absolutely beyond your control.
This might include everything from a terrorist attack to fluctuations in interest rates.

These tactics are straightforward and simple to grasp. The difficulty is that many investors fail to follow them in practice, instead allowing emotions to govern their decisions. You could end yourself going down that road as well. However, we will provide you with the tools you need to prevent it. It is entirely up to you whether or not you use them.

Averaging Costs in Dollars

The technique tries to avoid being influenced by market ups and downs. You never know if you're purchasing at the top or bottom of a market. We don't have a crystal ball, but what we can do is average out our investments over time. You may achieve this by employing a strategy known as dollar-cost averaging, which involves simply purchasing shares at regular intervals while disregarding price variations. The majority of stock market ups and downs are just noise. As a result, you should try to avoid thinking about them as much as possible. And, as previously said, stock prices fluctuate with bull and downturn markets. You reduce the tension (and hence the emotion) connected with these changes by using dollar-cost averaging. The expenses are averaged since you will occasionally purchase when prices are low and other times when prices are comparatively high.

In terms of increasing stock prices, this strategy may also help you avoid another emotional issue. Many investors get concerned when stock prices rise. They are concerned that share prices would soar to unprecedented heights that they will never fall again. They will "miss an opportunity" for profits and will be obliged to purchase shares at higher prices.

Short-term ups and downs don't matter in the long run.

Whether Amazon had a long gain four years ago or not is irrelevant to the dollar-cost-averaging investor. All that counts is the long-term trend--and buying shares on a regular basis along the way. In the chart below, we've used an arrow to highlight Amazon's long-term trend and circled a couple of the short-term variations that caused so much concern at the time. Traders most likely attempted to benefit from them. But notice how little they are in comparison to the broader image.

CHAPTER 24

DIVERSIFICATION

Diversification is the first approach employed when investing for the long term. Simply said, this is investing in more than one firm. Ideally, you would invest in many organizations from various industries and areas. The goal of using this method is to avoid sinking with a sinking ship.

However, a firm does not have to fail in order to damage its portfolio. Instead, it may stagnate, and a stagnated investment may be unable to provide you with the funds you want for a prosperous and secure retirement. You need investments that will expand over time.

Certain investments are unavoidably doomed to failure. A company's catastrophic collapse is unlikely to occur in the long run, yet it does happen from time to time. In most circumstances, a corporation will fall behind. Its stock price will stagnate or fall, even in absolute terms, rather than only in terms of where it should be to keep up with inflation. This is the most probable circumstance you'll face.

Some firms lose relative prominence while remaining solid investments. Intel, Microsoft, and IBM are a few examples. All three firms remain great investments, despite the fact that they are no longer the economic machines they once were.

Since quitting the PC sector, IBM has remade itself and followed numerous various avenues, focused on providing business services and machine intelligence, among other things. When it comes to specializations like AI, it remains a cutting-edge research organization, and although its stock isn't geared for fast development, it does demonstrate growth and pays a solid dividend payout. Microsoft continues to profit from the Windows operating system's dominance on desktop and laptop computers, but they have also expanded into areas such as cloud computing. Microsoft, on the other hand, has been left behind by the mobile wars and is no longer as vital as it once was. When it comes to major tech, you seldom hear Microsoft mentioned; instead, the spotlight is on Facebook, Amazon, Google, Netflix, and Microsoft's old adversary, Apple.

Does this imply that these businesses are unsuitable for investment? Certainly not. They would have been and continue to be strong assets to have in your portfolio, but they are instances of corporations that once appeared utterly powerful and indestructible but have matured into stable companies that are fine investments but no longer the toppers in the market.

However, as we've seen, some businesses--even formerly reputable ones--go bankrupt. GM required a bailout to escape bankruptcy, and if you had invested all of your money in GM in the years leading up to its downfall, you may have incurred significant losses. While organizations of that size are unlikely to collapse totally, it does happen from time to time, and you never know which companies may be affected five, ten, or twenty years down the line. As a result, it is critical to diversify your assets among a broad variety of organizations.

Industry sectors may potentially be dangerous. A certain industry or sector may sometimes have its own "bear market" when other sectors and industries are performing well. Furthermore, many industries may fade away or become obsolete over time. The coal sector may be moving in that way presently, but the horse and buggy whip businesses in the face of automotive growth are a classic illustration. Something so extreme is unlikely to happen very frequently, but the danger is always there, and you don't want to put all of your money into one enterprise.

The size of the company must also be considered. Companies are classified as large-cap, mid-cap, or small-cap. In addition, a "mega-cap" category has been added. The market capitalization of a firm is used to identify where it belongs. This is the price per share of the company's stock multiplied by the number of "outstanding" (marketable) shares. These are divided as follows:

Large-cap: A firm having a market value of $10 billion or more.
Mid-cap: These firms have a market capitalization ranging from $2 billion to $10 billion.
Small-cap: A small-cap firm has a market valuation of less than $2 billion.
Mega-cap: This category is intended for corporations valued at $200 billion or more, such as Apple and Google (Alphabet).
Micro-cap: Another often used classification, these are small-cap stocks with a market capitalization of less than $300 million. There are also "nano-cap" stocks with a market capitalization of less than $50 million.

Large-cap stocks are often steady, established businesses that generate dividends. Alternatively, they are enormous and fast expanding, such as Amazon and Netflix.

Small-cap funds have grown much faster than the S&P 500.

When deciding on an investment mix, the conventional guideline, though definitely not exclusive, is to consider mid-cap and small-cap companies to be riskier. A small-cap firm is significantly more likely to collapse, and it may not even make the headlines. As a result, investing in tiny, micro, and nano-cap enterprises may pose the most financial risk.

However, where there is danger, there is also significant opportunity for development.

A mid-cap or small-cap corporation has plenty of space for expansion. Many of them will be large-cap corporations in the future. Of course, determining which ones will play this function will be tough, but that is part of the investing game.

Another strategy to diversify is to divide your portfolio across firms with varying market capitalizations. You may allocate part of your funds to large-cap corporations, some to mid-cap companies, and so on. The amounts assigned to individual firms will be determined by your overall investing objectives.

In general, investors preferring lower investment risk and less aggressive growth will invest more, or perhaps all of their money, in large-cap corporations. Those looking for more aggressive growth and greater risk tolerance, on the other hand, will be ready to put more money into small and mid-cap enterprises. Of course, none of this constitutes hard and fast laws. Some of the firms we've discussed, such as Amazon, Apple, and Netflix, are both high-growth and large-cap stocks.

Tesla is another example; it is a large-cap company with enormous growth potential since few people have yet to purchase electric vehicles. It also carries a high level of risk; the company's objectives may never be realized.

If you want some growth potential in your portfolio, a diversification strategy should comprise roughly 15-20 firms dispersed throughout multiple sectors and industries, as well as a mix of large-cap, mid-cap, and small-cap company sizes. You don't want to have too many firms in your portfolio since it would be difficult to do adequate research and follow them to ensure that you have solid investments.

Many individuals seek to diversify their portfolios by investing in exchange-traded funds. But, for the time being, be mindful that exchange-traded funds may provide much greater diversification than investing in 10-20 firms on your own. One solution is to mix it up; maybe you invest in your top 10 favorite firms and then put the rest of your money into exchange-traded funds to diversify your portfolio.

The bottom line is that you want to build an investment portfolio that can withstand the failure of one, two, or potentially three firms in which you have invested. Of course, bear in mind that you may exit underperforming assets. If an investment is not assisting you in meeting your objectives, you should sell the shares as soon as possible and redirect your investment funds elsewhere. There are several situations that we may create to demonstrate the need for diversity. If you invest all of your money into coal firms, you could find that they are all bankrupt in 10 years. Alternatively, you may invest in roughly five small-cap firms and discover that one performs well over time, two lose value and two fail. That is not a long-term wealth-building strategy.

Instead, if you had invested in ten large-cap companies and five index funds in addition to your small-cap companies, the damage caused by the failing small-caps would have been limited and contained, and chances are the gains from your other investments would have vastly outpaced the losses.

Diversification also entails moving away from stocks.
Most investors will not want to invest solely in equities. You should also have part of your money invested in bonds, precious metals, real estate, and other assets. So, while developing your diversification plan, select what, if any, additional asset classes you want to include in your portfolio and then split them up by percentages. There are several online tools available from financial gurus and huge corporations like Vanguard and Fidelity that may be used as recommendations to decide how to manage your portfolio to accomplish various investing objectives.

CHAPTER 25

MINDSET AND PSYCHOLOGY

When it comes to investing, traders must have a certain attitude. Investing in stocks requires a great deal of self-control. To be successful in their investments, traders must get acquainted with a specific mindset. To get outcomes, a whole investment philosophy must be used. When investing in stocks, investors must separate themselves from their emotions; otherwise, they risk trading out of fear and greed. Investors must also avoid becoming too tied to any one investment. Although there is an art to investing, it is critical that investors use logic to guide their decisions.

Self-Discipline
When it comes to investing, self-discipline is essential. Investors must be able to stick to their strategies and accomplish their objectives. However, many investors are enticed by the prospect of higher performance and forsake all reasoning for the goal of generating higher returns on their assets. When it comes to market circumstances, they will rely on emotions. They may also incur higher expenses as a result of a lack of discipline. Regardless of the incentives, investors must adhere to their original strategy. In the long run, a short-term sacrifice will be worthwhile. Although it may not be the most pleasant option, the disciplined road is typically the most effective one, particularly in trading. Following the initial strategy and objectives established by the investor is critical.

Although there may be times when it is more advantageous to change plans due to a rapidly changing

129

market or personal financial disaster, it is generally best to adhere to the original plan. Once the investor deviates from the course, it will be much easy to repeat the action and forsake all initial goals.

The investor may respond irrationally and suffer significant losses. When this occurs, however, investors fail to recognize the long-term ramifications of their actions. Stocks that the investors should have kept may have resulted in profits, but the investor opted to lose money due to a lack of discipline.

The investor opens the door to allowing for loopholes whenever they see fit, and they end up hurting themselves in the long run. The investor should devise and adhere to a strategy on what to do if the market turns bad. They should make this strategy ahead of time so that they are not influenced in any way. The true discipline, however, is following through on this strategy when the time comes.

Investors should also be disciplined in their investment amount. Instead of opting at the last minute to spend the money they had put aside for stock on expenditures, they should adhere to their original plan. It is very simple to state that one will not invest this week and will return to it the following week, but they have already strayed from the plan. This might discourage the investor and lead to even more laxity in the future. The easiest approach to prevent this is to follow through on the strategy in the first place.

Investor should not alter their portfolio in response to recent market activity. This may be challenging, particularly during a bad market. However, it is typically worthwhile to persevere through difficult times and wait for another phase of progress. One's portfolio should be managed and rebalanced as needed. Although it may be tempting to adjust this depending on market circumstances, the investor must persevere through the difficult times. When investing for the long term, the investor must make certain that the investments are retained for the long run.

Investing Psychology
Several elements contribute to the psychology of trading. The trader must be able to maintain emotional control, make rapid judgments, and stay disciplined. Of course, this is in addition to being able to comprehend businesses and forecast stock price movements. Anyone can grasp the technical part of trading with enough practice and study. Those that grasp the psychological component of trading are the most successful. This is what distinguishes good traders from great traders. Trading psychology may be honed via experience, but it also requires a mental change on the part of the trader.

Traders must comprehend the emotions involved in trading. By first comprehending them, they will be able to become more skilled in dealing with such emotions. Traders must understand that anxiety is a normal reaction to poor stock market news. It is common for traders to feel pressed for time and be tempted to liquidate their holdings, minimize risk, or sell their assets.

This seems to be a smart decision at the moment. However, traders must make swift judgments that will profit them in the long run rather than gratify their emotions in the near term. They may incur losses as a result, but they will not lose out on the benefits that they would have missed had they succumbed to their emotions. Traders must understand that fear arises from what individuals perceive to be a danger to them. The danger in this case is to their money.

Investors must be able to fight greed in addition to fear. If an investor stays on a successful stock for too long, hoping to make as much money as possible, the gains may swiftly convert to losses. Long-term holding of a stock might be less rewarding than one would think. Once again, traders must devise a strategy ahead of time. They must understand when it is appropriate to sell a stock. It seems to the investor to be a good investment at the moment. They may earn more, perform better than they anticipated, and achieve greater profits. This happens from time to time.

Greed, on the other hand, is not always the best option. Traders must differentiate between greed and making sound judgments based on market movements. It is sometimes beneficial to deviate from the initial idea. However, emotion often interferes with rationality, and the investor makes a poor decision by listening to their heart rather than their mind.

Investors must devise a comprehensive strategy and establish ground rules for themselves. Instead of "going with the flow," it is critical for the investor's trading activities to have a step-by-step strategy. This should be based on intellectual conclusions rather than emotional or instinctual reactions. They must plan when they will join and when they will quit trades. This must be followed at all times, and it is an excellent technique to minimize emotional bias. Certain events may be planned for by the trader. If unexpected profits, whether favorable or bad, arise, the trader may create exceptions to their strategy. If specific macroeconomic circumstances occur, the trader may purchase security. They may also impose constraints in order to remove fear and greed. These should be the top and lower bounds. Upper bounds will reduce greed, while lower limitations will restrict fear. If such a limit is reached, the trader may suspend their actions for the day to prevent emotions from taking control.

Traders, on the other hand, should not justify their blunders. Although it is crucial not to focus on the past and all of the different ways in which the trader erred, the trader should acknowledge that they made errors. This is vital for self-improvement since the trader will always be able to perform their transactions more efficiently or successfully. As a consequence, the trader should absolutely study what went wrong every time they want to do so. This will increase the trader's future performance and decision-making abilities.

Mindset for Investing

Traders may also learn about various trading attitudes from other traders. There is a lot to learn through significant study and hearing how other individuals handle their trades. The investor's unfavorable emotional responses may be reduced by expanding their understanding. They will have a better understanding of the stock market and how it works, which will aid in the elimination of such responses.

Although it is critical to keep to one's strategy, traders must have a flexible mentality. They must be willing to experiment with new tools, buy and sell new stocks, investigate new businesses, and trade in unconventional ways. There is no such thing as a "correct" approach to trade. There are just several methods to do this. Some businesses may be more lucrative than others. Some may work well for one trader but not for another. Traders should be willing to experiment in order to determine the best approach for them to trade. When it comes to stock, this may also reduce the emotion.

Investors should also be critical of themselves and approach their trade with reasoning. Certain strategies for trading will provide higher profits. Traders must be willing to evaluate their performance and determine what worked and what did not. Traders must know that there is always space for development.

Perhaps the trader did not do extensive study for a period of time and overlooked some things that they should have spent more attention to. Perhaps the trader allowed emotion to affect their decisions. Recognizing possible poor habits allows the trader to concentrate on improving oneself and being a more lucrative and skilled trader in the future.

Traders must employ technical analysis to make investment choices. There are many approaches. Perhaps the trader prefers to concentrate on charts. This may be quite useful for getting a visual depiction of performance. The trader may have a group of investors from whom they seek advice on their transactions. They may keep a notebook in which to record their plans. There are programs available to assist with investing. Whatever method the trader decides to run their company, there should be some form of assistance to help them rationally assess their choices. A guide is required.

Emotional Separation from Stock
Trading and emotions just do not mix. Aside from greed and fear, traders must be willing not to get emotionally connected to their stocks. Stock investments are subject to continual fluctuation. There will be instances when it is prudent to invest in one stock but not another. However, traders often grow emotionally connected to a single asset. The investor must be able to let go of stocks that are no longer useful to them. There is no certainty that a stock will do well since the market and equities are continually changing. Investors must distance themselves from their stocks and understand when to sell them.

It is critical to separate logic from emotion while trading. Trading is a game of numbers. It all comes down to what will profit the trader in the long run. While it is easy to allow fear or greed to take over, to let past errors impair future success, or to grow emotionally connected to a specific stock, none of these are advantageous to one's performance. The trader must adopt a certain attitude and get acquainted with the right trading psychology. This will be quite advantageous to the trader.

CHAPTER 26

MARKETING STRATEGIES

Now that you know how to choose stocks, it's time to learn about the methods that may help you maximize your chances of making money from stocks. Take notice that stock returns are not guaranteed and, as previously stated, are subject to market risks, or the possibility of suffering losses due to negative movements or changes in stock prices. The best you can do is use tactics that reduce the risk and magnitude of potential losses while increasing your chances and quantity of rewards.

Set your profit target and stop-loss limits.
Emotions are one of the biggest adversaries you may have when it comes to stock market investing. Believe me when I tell you that in the past, my emotions had gotten the best of me when it came to trading stocks, and in most instances, those times ended in losses. As a result, having an objective foundation for your trading judgments is critical. One of them is determining your profit objectives.

If you want to trade on a regular basis, such as daily or weekly, a smaller profit target is preferable. A profit objective of 5% to 10% for a day or week is neither too high nor too low, and it is achievable with timely transactions. This implies that when the price of your stocks reaches the point where your projected profit (net of fees from purchasing and selling them) meets your profit target, you should sell the stock immediately. Don't let greed steal your profit, and regardless of how you feel, make a commitment to stick to your profit targets and sell when they're met. Because of the relatively long time period, you may strive for a significantly bigger profit objective if you use the longer-term, buy-and-hold technique.

Aside from establishing your profit targets at which to sell your stocks, you should also set a stop-loss limit, which is a price at which your maximum projected net loss--after deducting fees paid for both purchasing and selling the stock--is reached. What should your stop-loss limits be? It would depend on how much money you are willing to lose. If you're okay with losing 5%, make it a rule that when the price of your stock falls to a level where your projected net loss--after fees for purchasing and selling--will be 5%, you'll sell it.

Regardless matter how you feel, do it. It will help you progress more quickly. What is the purpose of a stop-loss order? Because not having such restrictions might exacerbate your losses. It's like jumping into an infinite hole. You may trade another day--or an hour--if you restrict your losses.

Averaging Costs
This is a method in which you lower the average buy price of your stock during downward moving markets, i.e., bear markets, to make it easier to profit later when the market flips back to an upward trend, i.e., bull market. This is how it works.

Assume you purchased ten shares of Apple, Inc. stock at $100 per share for a total cost of $1,000. Please keep in mind that since this is only an example, I have purposefully left out broker commissions and other minor charges.

Let's assume the price drops to $90 after a week. That gives you a loss of $10 per share, for a total projected loss of $100 or 10% (again, without including commissions and other expenditures for simplicity). There are two approaches you may take.

The first step is to wait for stock prices to rise by $10 to $100 a share so that you can break even. And if you want to earn a 5% profit, you'll need prices to rise to $105 per share.

Another option is to adopt the cost-averaging technique, which entails purchasing additional Apple, Inc. stock at the $90 price. Assume you purchased 10 additional shares at $90 each, which would cost you $900. You'll then have a total of 20 shares for a total cost of $1,900, and if you average that, your average purchasing cost per share will be $95 instead of $100. This is fantastic news!

Your average purchasing cost has dropped to $95 per share, you won't have to wait for prices to rise to $100 per share to break even. You must wait for it to rise to $95! Even better, when prices return to $100, you'll have made a profit of $100, or 5.26%.

If you want to go long-term, you may also employ the cost-averaging technique, also known as the buy-and-hold stock market investment strategy. Many individuals choose a really excellent stock, purchase it, and then purchase more when finances become available. When the market rises, they benefit automatically. When the market falls, they have an even better chance of increasing their future earnings and lowering their average buying expenses.

Selling on the cheap
Even when stock prices are falling, i.e., during a bear market, you may still earn money. How? Selling stocks, you don't own and then repurchasing them at substantially reduced prices. This is known as short selling. The term "short selling" refers to the act of selling stocks that you do not already own--you are "short of stocks!"

This is how it works.
Assume that the price of Apple's shares is falling. Assume it is presently trading at $95.00 per share, and based on technical analysis and market buzz, there is a very good likelihood that it will fall further to roughly $85.00 per share. You can sell 10 shares of Apple stock that you don't already own, then buy them back later in the day or week--depending on your arrangements with your chosen stock brokerage company--at a much lower price, such as $85.00 per share, for a profit of about $10.00 per share or a total profit of $100. You can do it even if prices are plummeting!

Short-selling can only be profitable when prices are falling.
You may be wondering, "Won't I go to jail for selling something I don't have?" You won't, since theoretically you won't be underpaying your counterparty. Because brokerage firms that allow short-selling include a securities loan facility, you may "borrow" shares of stocks that you don't have yet to sell on the market. When the price of the stock you short-sold falls further, you may buy it from the market to repay your broker for the shares you borrowed. It's as easy as that. That is why short-selling will not land you in prison!

Buy-And-Hold
The last trading method is the long-term approach, which is also known as a passive style of the stock market investment. In case you forgot, buy-and-hold techniques are called passive investing strategies since they require much less labor than active trading methods, which need constant market monitoring and trade execution. And, as the name indicates, all you'll need to do with this sort of investment approach is perform your initial study, purchase your stocks, and go about your business.

With a buy-and-hold strategy, you'll need to check your stocks at least once a month to stay current. If you check it once or twice a year, it won't damage you much since you're in it for the long haul, and market changes won't matter much. The most important--and possibly the most time-consuming--task you'll have to complete when using a buy-and-hold strategy is initial research. Because you will not be actively monitoring and managing equities under this strategy, you must choose companies that are fundamentally strong and have a solid financial basis for significant capital growth. Blue-chip stocks are often the best bets in this regard.

CHAPTER 27

KEEPING TRACK OF YOUR INVESTMENTS

Following your stock market investments, it is important to monitor and maintain track of these assets in order to understand how they are doing and if they are on track to reach your financial objectives. Monitoring also enables you to make better-educated judgments about whether to sell or keep your assets. We'll look at ways to keep track of your assets.

Stock Observation Activities

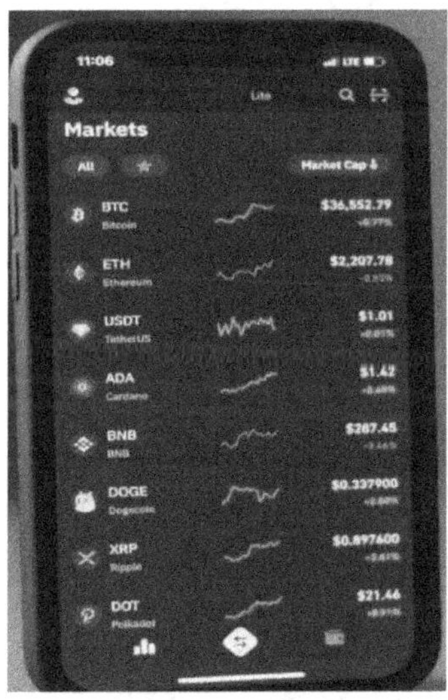

The following are some procedures you should take to monitor the equities in which you have an investment.

Tables of Stock

Stock tables are a terrific method to learn about your stock, its trading activities, value fluctuations, and other statistics. You should make practice checking them out. If you are investing for the long run, you should do this at least once a week. If you are a more active trader, you should review stock tables on a daily basis.

Compare Your Stock to Industry Benchmarks
Benchmarks are indexes that reflect a certain industry or the whole market. Benchmarks are used to demonstrate the overall performance of a certain industry or market. Checking how your stock performs in contrast to relevant benchmarks can inform you whether or not things are heading in the correct way. For example, if you discover that your stock is continuously doing worse than the benchmark for its sector, this is a sign that you should consider selling it.

Examine Your Account Statements
You should reread your broker's account statements frequently. As you do so, consider the performance of your assets as well as the fees you pay to your broker.
Remember that the fees you pay to your broker have a big influence on your profitability. You should also examine if the performance of your investments corresponds to your financial objectives.

Keep up with the latest company news.
Keep up to speed on any news impacting the firms in which you have invested. Read their news and press releases, visit their websites' noticeboards, and look for company-related news from third-party sources such as trade platforms, industry journals, news websites, and so on. When reading the news, keep an eye out for changes in senior management, mergers and acquisitions, and other business developments. Such information will offer you a sense of the company's direction, which will make it simpler for you to decide whether to hold or sell the company's shares.

You may set up Google alerts for the firms in which you have invested to make keeping up with corporate news simpler for yourself. This way, any news about these firms will be sent straight to your inbox.

Follow Economic News in General
In addition to news about the firms in which you have invested, you should keep up with market news and general events that may have an influence on the economy. Is the stock market in a bull or bear market? Is the nation experiencing inflation? What is the country's political climate like? Is a war on the horizon? How does the dollar do versus other currencies? All of these variables have an effect on the economy and the stock market, which means they have an effect on your portfolio as well.

Check Indicators for You
You should review the indications you used to determine the worth of your stocks before purchasing them regularly to see if there are any notable changes in these indicators. You may continue to own the stock if there are good improvements. If the adjustments are unfavorable, though, this is a hint that you should sell.

Examine the Quarterly Reports
As previously stated, publicly traded corporations are obligated to produce quarterly earnings reports. Take sometime after the reports are out to look through the reports of the firms in your portfolio. You may keep the stock if the reports indicate strong performance. If the reports reflect poor performance, this should raise concerns. However, don't sell your investments because of a single quarter's bad performance. Even the best-performing businesses encounter business downturns from time to time. However, if bad performance is frequently documented, it may be time to reassess the investment.

Reporting on Weekly Stock Performance
Most stockbrokers, particularly online brokers, will also offer you performance reports that show you how your assets have performed over time. You should look through these reports at least once a week. Most brokers, however, will enable you to specify the time period you want the report to cover, with time ranges ranging from a week to a number of years. The report will tell you the worth of your assets at the start of the time period as well as the current value.

These reports not only show you the success of your assets over time, but they also enable you to compare how your investments have done over time against a benchmark symbol. This enables you to see how your stocks are doing in comparison to the overall market.

CHAPTER 28

MONEY MANAGEMENT

The importance of money management in being a skilled trader cannot be overstated. When it comes to a person's day trading procedure, he or she must have a very strict money management system. Determine how much you are willing to risk and stick to it in your day-to-day trading attempts.

Day trading is already competitive, and computer-controlled algorithmic transactions are making it much more so. Many traders lose more money when they spend more in their day trading account, engage in short-term trading, or even gamble. Understanding market terminologies such as tender price, ask price, exit, and entrance price is critical for getting the most out of money management. As you get more knowledge and competence, you will be able to swap more profitably.

The age-old adage "plan your trade and trade your plan" is another critical stage in becoming a great trader. Because they limit your possibilities of losing money, your chances of profit are enhanced in every trade.

To maximize earnings from trading, always plan first, since it is well-known that if you fail to plan, you plan to fail. You will lose money if you lose faith in your abilities and trading plan, especially if you have a position in the market. You must handle trading such that you earn a profit at the end of the day despite any losses. You must understand how trading methods work throughout the day.

Despite the greatest instruments and trading tactics, a good trader must invest money and time. Many traders believe that by following some fantastic method, they can make money without putting in a lot of work. They must comprehend that rapacity, panic, and selfishness all lead to a stock market crash. It is preferable to study which trading strategy and market money management approaches work best for your trading style.

Important Trader Money Management Guidelines
As a trader, you must also control your financial load and make decisions based on your risk tolerance scale. The following money management guidelines may be followed to preserve your assets, increase returns, and minimize losses:

Experiment with Trade Sizing
Do not invest more than 10% of your stock trading capital in a single transaction. For example, if you have $25,000 in the capital, you may not put more than $2500 in any one of your trades.

Maintain Strict Stop-Loss Orders

On inventory valued more than $10, it is advisable to establish a minimum mental stop-loss of 10% and a hard stop-loss of at least 20%.

A mental stop-loss implies that your loss on a specific stock cannot exceed 10%. Assume you check your portfolio at the end of the day and see that one stock has lost more than 10%. You must next extensively examine the product and research the connected firm to determine what caused the price decline of your items. Hard stop losses, on the other hand, are valid stop orders made by traders. These are often used as a kind of insurance in the event of an unexpected change in market behavior.

Profits from Books

Partial earnings of 40% or above are ideal. It means that if the stock rises by 40% or more, you should sell a portion of it and save the remainder for future trading. In this manner, you may recoup a sum equal to or more than your original investment.

Profits That Follow

After achieving a 15% profit, move your stop-loss to the point of break-even and strive to accomplish it as long as you remain in that position; this is known as a trailing stop. Following the first 15% advantage, you will contemplate employing such a technique.

Avoid Trading on Margin.

It is critical to utilize margin trading with caution in order to avoid incurring a loss bigger than your original investment. When it comes to margins, they are normally a smart strategy to increase your wealth in main stocks. However, if not carefully examined and executed, such a stock investing strategy may swiftly result in massive losses. To summarize, the words of a well-known trader may be cited. He said that as one achieves larger positions, more challenges occur.

Small and Consistent Victories Race

Begin with little sums of money and gradually but surely increase your self-confidence and business account. Don't expect to get rich right now. If you have consistent trading returns over a lengthy period of time (more than a year), you might progressively raise your capital exposure, especially if you have stayed consistent even while the market is experiencing difficulties.

Diversify

Assume you have invested in 20 stocks using the rule of diversification and have only put 5% of your money in each company, and one of your options fails suddenly, resulting in a complete loss on that particular stock. This means that just 5% of your market earnings were squandered. You can subsist and trade without suffering major consequences. In contrast, if you do not have an efficient money management technique and your transactions are less diverse, committing your whole capital to single trades will keep your gains continuing, but most of your trading capital will be destroyed. You may potentially be removed from the exchanges entirely.

Manage Your Risk

If you are new to trading, it is recommended that you continue with a paper exchange practice program. Keep written records of your stock trading activities, as well as a record of all your emotions and mistakes. After roughly a month, you should be able to exchange with cash. Remember that big positions generate significant issues.

Limit orders may be used to enter and exit positions.

You may be given trading possibilities in the market; however, the price may vary from what you wish. A limit order placed close to the last close is usually filled since a stock usually retraces after the first portion of the session.

Some traders are unable to keep track of the stock throughout the day.

The market order is the answer to this dilemma. Please keep in mind that the price you have to pay may change after your purchase is completed.

The most common error investors make is mindlessly following a trading procedure. Regardless of the process's predetermined path, numerous factors must be considered.

Maintain an Eye on the Brokerage

Brokerage is the largest drain on your money, despite the fact that it is not taken seriously. A brokerage may entail hidden fees that eat into your earnings and increase your losses. Brokers might be selfish at times, concealing advantageous strategies for you while offering profitable schemes for them. This means that it is critical to individually investigate brokerage schemes rather than accepting the schemes supplied by the broker. Furthermore, the trading statement must be reviewed.

CHAPTER 29

COMMON ERRORS AND HOW TO AVOID THEM

As a newbie, the regulations of day trading may seem alien and difficult to understand. You want to make sure you're getting into the market and doing well, but you're also concerned that it will be too difficult to sustain and that the market will shift quickly. The market moves quickly, but there are many terrific tactics, including those discussed in this manual, that may help you get started.

Because of the quick movement of the market and the difficulty in predicting what will happen in the stock market, there are several errors that a newbie may make while working in this kind of market. These errors might cost the newbie a lot of money and cause them to be unable to participate in the market at all.

Simply because you are a novice does not imply that you must make some of these blunders. You only need to detect them and understand how to avoid them as much as possible. Throughout everything, keep in mind that even experienced traders make errors or have the market swing against them, causing them to lose money.

We can look at some of these typical errors and reduce them to a bare minimum, enabling us to save more money in the process. Some of the most typical errors novices make, and how to avoid them for greater success in day trading, are as follows:

Not Using Stop-Loss Orders

The first error we need to look at here is the stop-loss regulations. These are all about safeguarding you and ensuring that you maintain things secure in a market that is always changing. The stop-loss on one side ensures that if the trend changes, the market will take you out so you don't lose too much money. The stop-loss on the other hand ensures that you may exit with some profit before the rising trend reverses itself.

When a stock begins to fall in value, some rookie traders may panic because they perceive they are losing money. When they hit this stop-loss level, they elect to retain the stock rather than sell it. To assist preserve your investment, you should choose a stop-loss level and adhere to it no matter what. Sometimes the trend reverses and the money returns to you. Often, it will persist, and you will lose more money as a result. And it doesn't take long for a poor transaction to bankrupt you.

Set your stop-loss point before you begin the transaction and adhere to it. This helps you remove some of the emotions from the deal and allows you to exit. Sure, you'll lose money, but you'll lose a lot less than if you stick to the stock and don't sell in time.

These stop-losses are fantastic for ensuring that your emotions do not enter the trade. Everything is gone the moment such emotions join the game. When you attempt to work on your emotions, you don't make excellent judgments, but having those stop-losses in place ensures that you employ rationality before your emotions take over. If you wait until the deal has really begun, it is too late for the rationale.

Following the Trends
Another thing to be cautious of as a newbie in day trading is following trends. Many beginner traders believe that it is preferable to wait for some proof that they are correct before even considering starting a

position. This hesitancy may seem to be prudent, but it leads them to overlook some of the best entry opportunities. Even if they are correct, it may induce them to acquire a stock at a greater price than they desired.Find a strong technique that you understand and trust and wait for it to happen, but don't spend your time trying to keep up with the trend.

Not Anticipating Good Trades
As a beginner trader, you're undoubtedly eager to jump into the stock market and discover what you're capable of. You want to demonstrate that you understand what you're doing and that you can manage yourself in the fast-paced world of day trading. While it is nice to be enthusiastic along the journey, you must exercise caution. If you enter only because you are eager, you will almost certainly make a terrible deal along the line.

As a rookie day trader, you must be patient ahead of time to ensure that you obtain the appropriate transaction. And these fantastic day trading transactions may not appear straight soon. You must keep an eye on the charts and wait for some of the proper indications that technical analysis will reveal. Experienced traders understand that it is better to wait for the perfect transaction rather than pushing it or entering it all at the wrong price, which allows them to overtrade their accounts.

Not Making Your Own Rules and Following Them
When you start trading, a lot of things will change. Sometimes the rules are obvious and simple to follow, but other times the market seems to be chaotic. Whatever is going on with your trades or the market, you must spend some time developing and adhering to guidelines that you are comfortable with.

To avoid getting caught up in your transactions and all of the emotions that come with them (and allowing emotions to enter your trades may make it very difficult to perform well), you should create certain guidelines for each trade before it ever begins. This implies that you must have all of your entry and exit points in place before you join the transaction. And, once installed, do not turn them off.

Professionals that spend a lot of time in the stock market, whether via day trading or another method, understand that you may either concentrate on the transactions or on the regulations. You can't devote your time to both because you can't focus on both. Staying objective and following those criteria from the outset will allow you to retain complete control over your day trading.

It's Not Important to Forget the Fundamentals
Fundamental analysis is one of the approaches that you may utilize in numerous trading and investment alternatives. This is the method that enables you to examine all of the basic information about a business and then utilize that information to assess if a certain stock is a good one to buy. You would look into the company's management, its customers, its potential for growth, and its finances. However, since this is a long-term approach, it will not have many places in the day trader's plan.

New-day traders may get into the trap of looking at the firm and believing that if the company is excellent, it can never fail in this kind of trading. wonderful firms fail on a regular basis, and since you are only in the trade for a short time, it doesn't really matter how wonderful the company is. You just need them to perform well for the next several hours, and then they don't have to do anything. With day trading, there isn't much place for such fundamentals.

Traders who have worked with day trading know that how wonderful a company's fundamentals are will not matter since they will not be in the market long enough for this to show up. Instead, they look at how the market is doing and how it is anticipated to perform in the next few hours or fewer.

The expert investor understands that when the market is selling down, even solid business stock prices will fall. It is critical to disregard fundamentals in favor of following market signals and not worrying about anything else. This is a fantastic method for people dealing with long-term investments, but it is not suitable for day traders who have not been in the market for a long time.

CHAPTER 30

SOME OF THE STOCK MARKET'S TOP TRADERS BUFFETT, WARREN

When it comes to giving financial advice,few individuals can captivate an audience quite like Warren Buffet when it comes to financial advice. His amazing success in the field of investing, not to mention his $85 billion fortune, means that even individuals who aren't interested in finance sit up and take notice when Buffett gives his best wealth-building recommendations.

But Buffett is more than simply his financial balance (which is in the tens of millions of dollars). Despite his vast wealth, he is widely known for his generosity and frugality--he still lives in the same home in Omaha, Nebraska, that he bought for $31,000 in 1958, and he has recently pledged to give away 99% of his wealth to charities.To say the least, his narrative is interesting. Who exactly is Warren Buffet?

What are some of his ideals that you may implement in your personal and professional life? What can you learn about managing your life, money, and career from Buffett's personal experiences?

Buffett has already faced and conquered life's trials, paving the way for you to follow in his footsteps. All you have to do is be willing to pursue that route to achievement. You'll need to adjust and adapt it somewhat to fit your own needs and circumstances, but the framework is essentially in place. You may utilize the knowledge gathered by successful and affluent individuals who have built a name for themselves internationally as a roadmap to attain your own objectives in life and business.

Buffett has been a role model for hundreds, if not millions, of aspiring entrepreneurs and others, seeking to make a difference in their lives for decades. Because of his compassion and eagerness to assist others, his success has inspired the conduct of business people all around the globe and served as an exemplary benchmark to aspire for both professionally and personally. His impact is widespread, and even the world's wealthiest people have embraced Buffett's life philosophy. For example, because of Buffett's urging, more than 160 billionaires have decided to contribute and give up at least half of their money for charitable purposes.

Jones, Paul Tudor

Paul Tudor Jones is a philanthropist and hedge fund manager from the United States. Jones was born on the 28th of September, 1954. His enthusiasm for hedge fund management prompted him to establish Tudor Investment Corporation in 1980. The company's headquarters were and continue to be in Greenwich, connect cut, and it specialized in asset management. He then founded Tudor Group, a hedge fund holding company. Tudor was a hedge fund that specialized in the management of fixed income, currencies, stocks, and commodities.

His businesses have done well in recent years, earning him large fortunes. In February 2017, Forbes magazine estimated him to have a net worth of 4.7 billion, ranking him 120th among the 400 richest people in the world. Aside from that, Tudor 11 was ranked the 22nd highest and best-earning hedge manager in the world. Apart from concentrating on his hedge fund, Tudor has also shown a strong interest in humanitarian causes. This may be traced back to the situation when he established the Robin food charity just eight years after starting his hedge fund. This foundation is completely dedicated to eradicating poverty.

He was born in Memphis and spent most of his childhood there for education. This is because he went to the Presbyterian day school, then to an all-boys primary school, and then to Memphis High School. Jones attended Virginia University after graduating from high school, where he earned an undergraduate degree in economics in 1976.

He began working soon after completing his undergraduate degree since he was able to get employment at trading floors as a clerk the same year he graduated. He worked there for four years before being hired as a broker at E.F Hutton and Company in 1980. He worked for his new employer for nearly two years before leaving, expressing boredom with his employment. Jones intended to extend his education, and he applied to Harvard University's business school, however, he did not attend.

Jones Tudor was first assisted by his cousin, the EO of Dunavant Enterprises, a corporation recognized to be among the greatest cotton merchants in the world. William Dunavant connected Tudor to Eli Tullis, a commodities merchant who recruited Jones in his cotton company and still supervised him. He was educated in the trading and brokerage operations of the New York Stock Exchange.

According to Jones, Eli was the hardest and greatest trainer he had ever met, teaching him all of the attributes required to be a successful businessman. He taught him how to deal with market rivalry, and he also cautioned him that when you run a firm, you would constantly have ups and downs in your area of work.

Tim Cook's

Timothy Donald Cook is a business leader, industrial engineer, and developer from the United States. He presently serves as the Chief Executive Officer of Apple Inc. This is his current role at Apple Inc., where he previously served as Chief Operating Officer under founder Steve Jobs. In 1998, he joined Apple as the senior vice president of global operations, and then as the executive vice president of the globe in the department of sales and services. On March 24, 2011, he was elevated to Chief Executive Officer. He is remembered for his active advocacy of various human and environmental advancements, such as the reformation of political international and local surveillance, cybersecurity, corporation taxation both nationally and internationally, environmental preservation, and the American Manufacturing Act.

k went public with his sexual orientation and was named one of Fortune magazine's 500 CEOs. Cook also served on the board of directors of Nike-Inc., the National Football Foundation, and as a trustee of Duke University.

Around 2012, Apple Inc. agreed to compensate Cook with shares worth millions of dollars, vesting from 2016 to 2021. Cook said in a public statement that the proceeds from the given stocks will be donated to charitable organizations. This includes all he possesses.

Soros, George

George Soros was born György Schwartz on August 12, 1930, in Budapest, Hungary. Tivadar and Erzsébet Schwartz gave birth to him. The family was of Jewish heritage, but they opted not to follow their faith since anti-Semitism was on the increase in Hungary. They did not want their family to be suspected and investigated as an upper-middle-class family. To circumvent this, they renamed themselves Soros, which means "designated successor" in Hungarian. Soros' father preferred this name not just for its significance, but also because it was spelled the same forward and backward.

In March 1944, Nazi Germany invaded Hungary under the new name. The Nazis formed the Judunrat, a Jewish Council to which all Jewish youngsters were required to report. They could no longer attend their usual schools. This body was responsible for deporting any Jews discovered in Hungary. They chose school-aged youngsters to deliver the deportation notifications to the individuals.

Soros was 13 years old at the time and had received paperwork to present to Jewish attorneys. Tivadar, his father, encouraged him to tell the individuals as he distributed them that if they showed up to work, they would be deported.

During this perilous period, deception was required to safeguard many Jewish individuals. Soros' parents concealed their Jewish ancestry once again by acquiring paperwork stating their "Christian" beliefs.

This enabled them to endure the Nazi takeover. For his own safety, young George had to pretend to be the "godson" of a Hungarian government figure. George was sent to accompany this officer to a Jewish family's estate to take inventory. He wasn't a part of the process, but he had to observe it. Because his wife was Jewish, the official who was defending Soros had a direct link to the Jewish community. At this time, she had already gone into hiding.

Many Jewish persons in Hungary were protected as a result of measures like these. Soros's father's attempts to aid people during this period cemented in young Soros's view that his father was a great hero and a defender of the Jewish people.

The Nazi control of Hungary ended in 1945, bringing an end to the concealment. Soros was able to flee Hungary immediately after the Nazis were defeated in 1947. He may now continue his schooling in London. He moved to England and studied philosophy at the London School of Economics under philosopher Carl Popper. He obtained his Bachelor of Science in Philosophy in 1951. He graduated with a Master of Science in philosophy in 1954.

CHAPTER 31

DOS AND DON'TS OF STOCK MARKET
"DO" YOUR RESEARCH

Here are some of the dos and don'ts of stock markets that you should keep in mind while making your investments.

The first step is to do an extensive study on the issue. You must understand what some of the phrases mean and what you must do to create profitable investments. You must do more research online. You may also look for excellent publications in other places.

There is no such thing as too much knowledge, and the more you read, the better. You will also need to purchase a simple handbook that will show you how to use the software you will be using to buy and sell stocks. Everything from accessible broker companies to national economies to current news and computerized trading choices will need investigation. Being well-versed in the technological aspects of trading would be quite beneficial to you.

Because most brokers have their own trading software, each program for each broker will vary somewhat. Exchanges often design their own software, known as matching engines, so if you trade on several exchanges, you will notice subtle discrepancies. Make sure you understand the distinctions so you don't make errors while switching from one exchange to another.

When accessing the exchanges electronically, you normally have two options: the GUI (graphical user interface) and the API (application programming interface). The GUI is an exchange-provided interface that can be downloaded to your computer, while the API is your own interface that will connect with the exchange software. If you work with various exchanges and brokers, having your own API might help you keep all of the information in one place. Third-party APIs are often offered for purchase. Unless you are an expert in software creation, it is advisable to buy a pre-built system or utilize the system offered by your broker.

Keep a Journal
Before you begin investing in the stock market, you must do research and choose companies that you believe will perform well. Look for those that will show to be profitable long-term investments. If you want to day trade, seek penny stocks, which will increase and decrease in value in a short period of time. You should always keep a diary to assist you to document your day-to-day stock market transactions. This may be done in writing, but an electronic diary is better since

It is also beneficial to separate your study journal from your purchasing and selling diary. One should be used to monitor equities in which you are interested, even if you do not own them, and the other to record any investing transactions, regardless of the instrument or whether you are buying or selling.

It is easy to get carried away, and many individuals make the error of not keeping track of how much they spend and where they spend it, so a trade ledger will be just as useful as a diary. Again, an electronic ledger is the greatest solution since it can readily provide you with the most up-to-date information without requiring you to do computations after every single transaction or sale.

It is also critical to have a strategy in place to keep you from overspending. It is a good idea to create and stick to a monthly budget for the investments you will make in a month to guarantee that you spend wisely. The ideal budgeting strategy is to split your money by investment category—a certain amount for equities, mutual funds, precious metals, and so on. This guarantees that your portfolio stays diverse and that you do not spend all of your money in one spot and subsequently lose your whole month's investment. An electronic ledger will also be the best alternative for budget computations.

Risk Capital "Do"
Risk capital is money that you are prepared to put at risk. It is capital that you should individually possess and cannot be owned by anybody else. Risk capital is also useful for people who like taking market risks, such as investing in penny stocks. Remember that the criteria for day trading are that 25% of your investments must be backed up by risk money. It is better to maintain your risk capital separate from your other savings in a different bank account. This will protect you from exceeding your budget and squandering all of your resources.

Borrowing money from someone else and investing it in the market is not considered risk capital since you will not be confident in your investments and will always question whether you made a mistake. As a result, it is critical that you only invest money that belongs to you and no one else. In most circumstances, it is also prudent not to invest for someone else since they may have different expectations than you.

"Do" Portfolio Diversification
You need a bit of this and that in it so that the danger is spread out. Some consumers are unaware that placing all of their money into the same security doubles or

triples their risk, since one simple error may result in the loss of all of your risk capital.

As a result, it is essential to invest in equities, precious metals, foreign currency, commodities, and so on.

At the same time, it is critical to diversify within each of these categories in order to further spread risk. For example, you must invest in several companies from various sectors, such as the agricultural, technological, and energy sectors. Commodities may be treated similarly. A well-diversified portfolio may include gold, a retail firm, a renewable energy production company, wheat, coffee, and a foreign currency such as the Japanese Yen.

"Do" Seek the Advice of Experts

It is a good idea to seek the advice of a professional. Some individuals may find it difficult to invest in the stock market. There will be uncertainties and fears that must be overcome in order to make profitable investments. You may enlist the assistance of specialists in your life to accomplish this. If you know someone who trades in the stock market, you may not even need to pay for guidance; just hunt them up and request their opinion.

They should be able to help you with your investments. Examine their trading style and the stocks they choose. They could even let you sit in on a trading day with them. Take close notes and try to answer as many of your questions as possible. Are they keeping assets for a long period or selling them quickly? What exchanges and trading platforms do they employ? What is their daily or monthly spending limit? Do they have a specific target for the return on their investment? These are some of the questions you should consider answering.

Stock Market Dos and Don'ts
Here is the several don'ts to keep in mind while investing in the stock market.

Don't Imitate Someone Else
While seeking guidance from others will help you get more understanding, don't duplicate another person's financial ideas since they will vary for each individual. You must create an individualized approach for yourself rather than just replicating what works for others. Even if they are thriving, you must stay with whatever best matches your investing style. Keep in mind that every transaction and sale have an effect on the market.

Even though your investment seems tiny at first, it has an effect. You can take inspiration from other people's patterns, but it's better not to replicate what they're doing since it may not work for you in the same manner. If you like their options, you may ask them to advise you and create an investment strategy for you. It's never a terrible idea to run your financial ideas by a professional.

Make No Hasty Decisions
Never hurry into a choice because you will make a mistake.Take your time with everything, particularly if you want to stay involved for a long period. To gain the full advantages of anything, you must be completely certain of it. Before investing in a stock, wait and monitor it for at least a month. Invest in it if you are satisfied with its performance.

This is particularly difficult if you want to undertake day trading. The greatest advice would be to first obtain some expertise in long-term investing and then work your way down with your time restriction. Even day traders spend hours studying and examining companies that they may only hold for a minute or two, but every one of them will tell you that it was well worth their effort.

Ignore the News

Don't overlook stock market news. Daily newspaper reading is required to determine which stocks are suitable for investment and which should be avoided. You must determine the market mood by examining patterns. Many individuals underestimate the importance of going through the recommended stock columns, believing that it will not work for the general public, but it will if you make the appropriate choices.

Never make an investment without first reading the day's news. This may seem to be tiresome at first, but once it becomes a habit, you will find it extremely pleasurable. Your knowledge base will begin to expand and multiply, making trading much simpler. Remember that investing is not like riding a bike, where you may not have ridden it in years and then hop on it and ride it like you never stopped. No, investing knowledge must be kept up to date. If you take a year or two off from investing, you will need to rebuild your whole knowledge set.

Don't Put Your Trust in Message Boards

It is not wise to trust message boards uncritically since they may include incorrect information. To choose the finest stocks for yourself, you must do your own study. If you end up believing other people's recommendations and buying terrible stocks, you will come to despise the stock market. So, use caution when selecting stocks based on what message boards have to say about them. Everything should be taken with a grain of salt. Once you start investing, you'll realize that your greatest counsel is your own gut and intuition, which is fueled by information.

Tock market investment is one of the best ways to protect your hard-earned money. During the recession, most businesses struggled to keep their heads above water, and the majority of average individuals began to save to avoid irreparable loss. Most regular stock purchasers began to walk away from the market, but fewintelligent people acquired the shares at an unbelievablelower price. When the stock value of a large corporation falls, you may acquire the stock for a lower price, and it is the best moment to buy shares.

CONCLUSION

Stock market investing is no longer a secret, owing to the internet age, which allows you to set up your account from home and begin a new manner of investing in the stock market. People used to have to chase after the share brokers to find out the value of their shares and to look at their account details. But nowadays, everything is transparent, and you can look at your account data and the most recen

t price of the stock while sitting comfortably at home.
Only one thing is certain, and that is change. Change is always definite, as is the experienced stock world. It hasmovedintocyberspacefrom the cluttered, clumsy stock markets, which still look like fish markets. The growth of the Internet is the cause of the revolution in stock markets and another trading.

It has an easy access feature as well as the convenience of operating stock from one's office or home. The peedy technology acted as a trigger to disrupt the stock market norm. It is no longer an alien world for people. Rather, it was discovered, and the myterioune This trading location has just disappeared. People are now more comfortable trading online, and investors and their investments have increased threefold. The bull and bear are no longer contained to the creams but have been skimmed to the common.

since a stock market investor, you should keep an eye on the market trend and be prepared to face a downfall at any moment, since the risks in this company are fairly large and severe in certain cases.

Before investing your money in the stock market, you need to learn about the firm and market trends. The company's future goals and objectives might be very useful in making the proper decision.

Fatigue is accompanied by an amazing feeling of accomplishment at the conclusion of a well-run marathon. All of the planning, fretting, and training in all kinds of weather seemed to have been worthwhile. Not simply "worth it," but a priceless experience that, in my opinion, makes one a better person.

A well-managed financial strategy provides the same feeling of success; long-term preparation and patience pay off. You set your objectives and attained them: a college education for your children and a nice retirement for you. Furthermore, if you invest effectively enough, you may opt to contribute part of your gains to organizations and causes you to believe in, making you a better person and the world a better place.

Equally essential, you will have control over your money. You will acquire used to the market's and individual stocks' ups and downs. You intend to invest in high-quality dividend-paying equities for the long term. You'll be aware of what may go wrong, but you'll also be aware of how much can (and probably will) go well. Perhaps you never imagined you'd be able to achieve it. Now that you know you can, why not give it a try?

www.ingramcontent.com/pod-product-compliance
Lightning Source LLC
LaVergne TN
LVHW041317200726
843509LV00009B/521